Celebrating the Easter Vigil

Celebrating the Easter Vigil

Edited by Rupert Berger
and
Hans Hollerweger

Translated by Matthew J. O'Connell

A PUEBLO BOOK

The Liturgical Press Collegeville, Minnesota

Design: Frank Kacmarcik

The Publisher gratefully acknowledges the Reverend Ronald F. Krisman for his selection of English-language music for the Vigil.

Originally published in German as *Dies ist die Nacht* © 1979 Verlag Friedrich Pusted, Regensburg.

Contents

Preface vii

Preface

There can be no doubt that the reform of the Easter Vigil, introduced more than a quarter of a century ago by Pius XII, has been a source of greater spiritual profit for us. The celebration of Easter has become the focal point of the liturgical renewal, and there has been a growing awareness, at least in the base communities, that Easter, the feast of the Lord's resurrection, is the "feast of feasts."

On the other hand, the possibilities latent in the celebration of the Easter Vigil do not yet seem to have been fully exhausted. For this reason, in October 1977 the Liturgical Commission of Austria sponsored a symposium on the Easter Vigil, which was held at the St. Virgil Formation Center in Salzburg. The lively interest shown by all the participants made it clear that, on the one hand, the faithful have given a positive reception to the Easter Vigil, but that, on the other, there is need of more effectively integrating the celebration into the life of the community. The most important requisite to this end is a deeper spiritual understanding. A great help to such an understanding will be a more intensive homiletic explanation during Lent and the Easter season. Care must also be taken in the future to assure that the principles of liturgical theology become the norm for all efforts at an improved celebration.

The participants in the symposium also agreed that the most pressing task is not to bring about structural change, but to take advantage of the very useful rite we now have. It was felt as a clear defect that the Easter

Vigil has too few ties with traditional and new customs, and therefore has still not taken real root in the life of the people. In any case, the hope is for a more strongly experiential celebration which will bring home to the faithful the true dimensions of the content of this feast.

I am happy that the papers of the Salzburg symposium and the results of the discussion there are being made available to a wider circle. May these fruits of the experience of pastors and of all who contribute to the celebration of the feast prove helpful, so that "of all the days on which devout Christians offer their worship in many forms, none may stand in higher esteem than the feast of Easter which seals the dignity of all celebrations in the Church of God" (Leo the Great).

Archbishop Karl Berg
President of the Austrian Liturgical Commission

I. Foundations

Notker Füglister

The Biblical Roots of the Easter Celebration

Since the Second Vatican Council, at the latest, the concept "Easter mystery" has become a theological slogan and password. In very diverse texts the Council speaks repeatedly of the *mysterium paschale* or "paschal (Easter) mystery." The phrase means that the Easter mystery of the passion, death, and resurrection of Christ is the accomplishment of the redemptive work that had been foreshadowed in the Old Testament and consists in the conquest of death and the communication of life. Therefore the Easter mystery is also the origin of the Church and sacraments, especially of baptism and the Eucharist (SC 5 and 61; cf. 10 and 47). Christian life thus has a paschal character; it is a sacramental and existential sharing and participation in the paschal mystery of Christ. Christians are incorporated into this mystery through baptism and the Eucharist (SC 6); on the basis of the close link thus established with the Christ event (which to a certain extent lays hold even of non-Christians), they are to imitate this mystery in their own "profane" everyday lives (GS 22; cf. 38 and 52), as the saints, for example, have imitated it (SC 104).

This imitation is facilitated through the liturgy, of which the two central actions—the weekly Sunday Eucharist and the annual feast of Easter—celebrate the paschal mystery and render it present and operative (SC 106–7, 109; cf. 102). The first and most important task of bishops and priests is to help the faithful know and live this mystery (OT 8; CD 5; cf. AG 14).

"CHRIST, OUR PASCHAL LAMB, HAS BEEN SACRIFICED"

The concept of "paschal mystery" occurs first around 160 in Asia Minor. In his work *On the Pasch*, which is the oldest surviving Easter homily, Melito of Sardis speaks repeatedly of the "mystery of the pasch" as well as of the "mystery of the Lord." This mystery is "both old and new: old in its prefiguration, new in its grace."[1] Melito's mystagogical sermon is of great value for the history both of the liturgy and of theology; it is, moreover, very much to the point even today. It begins with the words: "The scriptural account of the Exodus of the Hebrews has been read, and the words of the mystery have been proclaimed: how the lamb was slain and the people were saved." What we have therefore is a homily on the Passover pericope that has just been read from the Book of Exodus. (N.B. For Melito "scripture" still means the Old Testament; our "New Testament" had not yet acquired canonical status as part of the Bible.) In the Christian community, therefore, the texts being read and explained were the very ones that formed the nucleus of the Jewish Passover liturgy (the Passover Haggadah) and were read by the head of the house during the domestic Passover celebration or Seder.

In addition, since Melito evidently belonged in the Quartodeciman tradition, his Easter homily was delivered on the late evening of the 14th Nisan, that is, on the same day and at the same hour as the Passover meal was being celebrated in Jewish homes. And yet, surprisingly, nothing is said of the Last Supper; Melito speaks only of the passion and death of Jesus, which had supposedly taken place at the hour when Israel was celebrating the Passover: "And so you put your Lord to death on the great feast day. You rejoiced, but he hungered; you drank wine and ate bread, but he drank vinegar and gall; your faces were bright, but his grew dark; you were full of jubilation, but he was in tribula-

4

tion; you sang songs, but he cried out. . . ; you lay at
ease on soft couches, but he lay in the tomb and his
grave-clothes."[2] For "what does 'Pasch' mean? The
name is derived from the event: 'Pasch' is from 'passion.' " (Philo of Alexandria had already connected
Pascha, the Grecized form of the Aramaic *Pischa*, with
the Greek verb *paschein*, "to suffer.")

But the crucified Jesus is also the risen Lord: "But he
rose from the dead and ascended to the heights of
heaven." He is "the immortal Lord who like the lamb
was not broken (cf. Ex 12:46) but arose as God." As the
one who on the cross was exalted by the Father, he is
present in the midst of the celebrating community: "I
am your forgiveness; I am the Pasch of salvation; I am
the lamb sacrificed for you; I am your baptism; I am
your life; I am your resurrection; I am your light; I am
your salvation; I am your king.'" Cross and resurrection, Good Friday and Easter Sunday, belong together;
they constitute the one paschal mystery and are commemorated by one and the same feast.

The many correspondences with the theology, ter-
minology, and chronology of the gospel of John are obvious. "The Lamb of God, who takes away the sins of
the world" (Jn 1:29) is here the passover lamb: Jesus,
who like the passover lamb did not have a single bone
broken (Jn 19:36 = Ex 12:40), dies, according to the
fourth gospel, at the very hour when in the nearby temple all the lambs were being slaughtered and offered in
sacrifice in order that a short time later they might be
eaten at the Passover supper in the homes of Jerusalem.
This parallelism, which is probably the work of the
evangelist himself, is based on one of the earliest
soteriological interpretations of the death of Jesus. For
when Paul says to the Corinthians in about the year 55
that "Christ, our paschal lamb, has been sacrificed" (1
Cor 5:7), he is making his own a formula already in
existence (cf. 1 Pet 1:18–19).

5

In the mind of the Johannine Jesus, the Jewish Passover was the "hour" which the Father had appointed from eternity and toward which Jesus was consciously moving throughout his earthly life: "Now before the feast of Passover, when Jesus knew that his hour had come to depart out of this world to the Father, having loved his own who were in the world, he loved them to the end" (Jn 13:1). On the evening before his death he washed the feet of his disciples during a farewell meal with them. The synoptic gospels too tell us of this farewell evening meal. But according to them the meal took place "on the night when he was betrayed" (1 Cor 11:23), that is, not on the 13th Nisan but on the 14th. For according to the unanimous testimony of the three older gospels the meal was a Passover meal: "And when the hour came, he sat at table, and the disciples with him. And he said to them, 'I have earnestly desired to eat this passover with you before I suffer'" (Lk 22:14–15). Whatever the historical fact may have been (the Synoptic chronology seems more probable[3]), the important thing from the theological standpoint is that the institution of the Eucharist and, with it, the interpretation and actualization of the Christ event take place in the framework of an Old Testamental and Jewish Passover meal. This means that the Old Testamental-Jewish theology and liturgy of Passover were and remain the true horizon within which to understand the New Testamental and Christian paschal msytery.

MEMORIAL CELEBRATION AND SACRIFICIAL MEAL
The Jewish Passover owed its origin to two originally distinct celebrations that had already been fused into a single unit in pre-Christian times: the Passover celebration which was held at night (Pesach) and a week-long festival of unleavened bread (Mazzoth). I cannot here take the time to trace the complicated development of these two feasts,[4] but must settle instead for sketching the structures which are relevant to theology and

liturgy.[5] In this context three aspects deserve special attention.

First: Passover was essentially a memorial celebration: "This day [or: the custom of eating unleavened bread] shall be for you a memorial day" (Ex. 12:14; cf. 13:3). In proclamation (in the Haggadah) and praise (especially in the form of the Hallel, i.e., Pss 113–18), Jews remembered the foundational saving deeds of God and the salvation which these brought to all Israel and to each individual Israelite. But this kind of liturgical anamnesis or "remembering" was not simply a calling to mind of an event now historically past; rather, as seen in the light of the biblical concept of remembering, it was a rendering present, both subjectively and objectively, of the event being commemorated, and this both in the celebrating Israelite and in the God being celebrated. This meant that in each successive present celebration, the salvation connected with Passover was rendered effectively present and operative for the celebrating Israelites: *"This day* you are to go forth," and therefore the rite is accomplished "because of what the Lord did for *me* when *I* came out of Egypt" (Ex 13:4, 8). Or, in the words of the Haggadah:

"In every generation a man must so regard himself as if he came forth himself out of Egypt. . . . Therefore are we bound to give thanks, to praise, to glorify, to honor . . . him who wrought all these wonders for our fathers and for us. He brought us out from bondage to freedom. . . ; so let us say before him the Hallelujah."[6]

In a similar manner, the New Testament celebration of the Eucharist takes place amid thanksgiving and proclamation as a kerygmatic-eucharistic anamnesis or remembering (cf. 1 Cor 11:23–27; Lk 22:19), in which God's foundational act of salvation, accomplished in Christ, becomes present and operative.

Second: In this Easter anamnesis there is no question of

a simple mental and verbal remembering; rather there is a symbolic-real *ritual re-presentation*. The Easter vigil (which, as "the mother of all holy vigils" [Augustine], is the origin of the Christian vigil service) corresponds to the vigil which Yahweh and the Israelites kept at the first Passover (Ex 12:42). The travelers' garb (Ex 12:11) and the peaceful reclining at the table during the Jewish Passover represent respectively the readiness for departure and the liberation from slavery.

In particular, the individual components of the meal have a commemorative function, and the interpretation of them serves as a point of departure for the kerygmatic and catechetical approach (in addition to the Haggadah cf. Ex 12:26–27; 13:7–8). Thus the unleavened bread ("the bread of affliction") together with the bitter herbs symbolize slavery (Deut 16:3) but also the hasty departure (Ex 12:34, 39). In addition, this bread, together with the wine, which is not mentioned in the Old Testament but played an important part in the Jewish Passover, also points to the goal of the journey: the entrance into the Promised Land (Josh 5:10ff.). Furthermore, the bread and wine, over which the host pronounced the praise of God (the "blessing"), would be interpreted by the guests who shared them not only as the embodiment and expression of fraternal communion but also as in a sense the bearer and communicator of blessing. Here again it is worth noting the correspondence to the New Testament Eucharist which likewise is an "action." Here too bread and wine serve both as memorial and as bearer of salvation (cf. 1 Cor 10:14–22 and 11:23–32).

Third: The Old Testamental-Jewish Passover was also a sacrificial meal. Once the worship of Israel had been centralized, the lamb to be eaten at home during the "post-Egyptian" Passover was first, like all other saving victims, offered in sacrifice in the temple. The father of the family or his delegate slaughtered the lamb; then the priests offered to Yahweh the part belonging to him

8

by burning the fat of the animal on the altar and pouring its blood over the altar. This ritual gave expression to the ideas of communion and covenant: God and human beings took part in one and the same meal. According to late Old Testamental and Jewish views, the blood of the Passover lamb, like all blood offered in sacrifice, had an expiatory value: it could wipe away the sins of those on whose behalf the lamb was sacrificed.[7] Against this background we can understand the idea of sacrifice that is connected with the New Testament Eucharist (cf. 1 Cor 10:14–22) and especially the saving value that is assigned to the blood of Jesus ("the blood of the lamb": 1 Pet 1:18–19; Rev 5:9, 12; 7:14; 12:11; cf. Jn 19:34, 36), in particular in the context of the Eucharist, where the blood of Jesus is "my blood of the covenant, which is poured out for many for the forgiveness of sins" (Mt. 26:28).

A COMPENDIUM OF SALVATION HISTORY

As we have seen, the Old Testamental and Jewish Passover was essentially a commemorative celebration. At its heart was the foundational, central Exodus event, which supplied the real biblical etiology (or "causal-explanatory story") of Pesach-Mazzoth (Ex 12). But according to the explicit testimony of the Old Testament itself, in addition to the Exodus from Egyptian slavery, the entry into the Promised Land which concluded the Exodus was also a Passover event (Josh 5). Yahweh was and remained the "God of the Exodus" (Ernst Bloch), that is, the God who in the past of salvation history, the present of each age, and the eschatological future still to come leads his people out, through, and into, and does so through the Passover and in the form of a Passover.

But Judaism also regarded a whole series of other saving events in the Bible as Passover events, so that Passover became increasingly a compendium of salvation history. In the present context a midrash which in substance goes back to pre-Christian times deserves our special attention. It occurs in the Palestinian targums on

Ex 12:42, which reads: "It was a night of watching by
the Lord, to bring them out of the land of Egypt; so this
same night is a night of watching kept to the Lord by all
the people of Israel throughout their generations."
(Note the mutual character of the Passover watching:
Yahweh watches over Israel during the night, while Israel for its part keeps watch for Yahweh as it waits for
him.) Here is what our Jewish *Exsultet*, or Easter hymn
of praise, has to say[8]:

"It is a night reserved and set aside for redemption to
the name of the Lord at the time the children of Israel
came out redeemed from the land of Egypt.

"Truly, four nights are those that are written in the
Book of Memorials.

"The *first night*: when the Lord was revealed over the
world to create it. The world was without form and void
and darkness was spread over the face of the abyss (Gen
1:2) and the Word of the Lord was the Light, and it
shone; and he called it the *First Night*.

"The *second night*: when the Lord was revealed to Ab-
ram, a man of a hundred years, ⟨between the pieces⟩
[i.e., at the concluding of the covenant; cf. Gen 15:17–
18], and Sarah his wife, who was a woman of ninety
years [at the time when the birth of Isaac was an-
nounced; cf. Gen 17:17]. . . . And Isaac was thirty seven
years when he was offered upon the altar. The heavens
were bowed down and descended and Isaac saw their
perfections and his eyes were dimmed because of their
perfections (Gen 22:1–14; cf. 27:1), and he called it the
Second Night.

"The *third night*: when the Lord was revealed against
the Egyptians at midnight (Ex 19:29): his hand slew the
first-born of the Egyptians and his right hand protected
the first-born of Israel to fulfill what the Scripture says:
Israel is my first-born son (Ex 4:22). And he called it the
Third Night.

"The *fourth night*: When the world reaches its end to be redeemed: the yokes of iron shall be broken and the generations of wickedness shall be blotted out; and Moses will go up from the desert and the king Messiah from on high. One will lead at the head of ⟨a cloud or:⟩ the flock and the other will lead at the head of ⟨a cloud or:⟩ the flock and his Word will lead between the two of them, and . . . they will proceed together.

"This is the night of the Passover to the name of the Lord: it is a night reserved and set aside for the redemption of all the generations of Israel."

Here we have the biblical roots of the feast of Easter. The unbroken continuity between the Old Testamental and Jewish Passover and the New Testamental and Christian Easter is indeed astounding. We need think only of the Old Testament readings for the Easter Vigil: their choice and significance can only be understood in the light of their Jewish background and use. This fact is of great practical importance for our preaching and catechesis. If we want to understand, and help others to understand, the whole depth and height, length and breadth of the paschal mystery that is identical with the mystery of Christ, we must in our preaching come to terms with the relevant Old Testament texts and themes.[9] In what follows I shall therefore go briefly into the Passover events in the history of salvation and indicate the theological motifs implicit in them.

THE GOD OF THE EXODUS

"Let my people go, that they may serve me" (Ex 8:1) is the message Yahweh has Moses deliver to Pharaoh. For "I have seen the affliction of my people who are in Egypt, and have heard their cry because of their taskmasters; I know their sufferings, and I have come down to deliver them out of the hand of the Egyptians, and to bring them up out of that land to a good and broad land, a land flowing with milk and honey" (Ex 3:7–8). This liberation, which according to the Old Testament is the origin and explanation of Passover and therefore is at the center of the Jewish Passover proclamation, has three phases: the warding off of death from Israel (or its first-born) by means of the blood of the Passover lamb that is used as a protective sign (Ex 12:13, 27); the directly ensuing conduct of Israel out of Egyptian slavery (Ex 12:42; 13:8); and the passage of the Sea of Reeds as a further rescue from death and as definitive liberation from affliction (Ex 13:17 to 15:21). The following points are particularly important in relation to the New Testament and the Christian understanding of Easter.

1. Insofar as it is a departure, a going forth, the Exodus initiates a *movement of salvation* into which the human beings now liberated by God are drawn: they are sent forth on a journey and thereby brought to a goal (cf. the archetypal image of "life's journey"). In this process the being-led-out (from Egypt) becomes a being-led-through (through the Sea of Reeds and then through the wilderness); the leaving becomes a breakthrough; the Exodus (or going forth) becomes a *diabasis* (or passing over). That is how the Hebrew *Pesach* is interpreted by Philo of Alexandria, who was to have such an important influence on patristic exegesis, especially in regard to this very point. The Passover sacrifice thus becomes a *diabatērion*, that is, a passage sacrifice or passing-over sacrifice such as people used to offer in antiquity on various occasions, including the crossing of a river.

In this way the "liberative passing-over" of the Israelites replaces the original "protective passing-over" of Yahweh (Ex 12:23, 27) as the real theme of the feast. In the Old Testament itself, then, there is already question of a passing over from Egyptian slavery to the freedom of God's children, from the service of Pharaoh to the service of God, from darkness to light, from death to life. Consequently the Old Testament Passover has already become a celebration of life.[10] The closeness to New Testament thinking is clear. I need only mention the gospel of John, according to which on Passover Christ passes from the world to the Father, and Christians must in their turn accomplish the same passage from death to life (Jn 13:1, and 5:24; cf. 1 Jn 3:14).

2. A further motif that will be taken over by the New Testament is the motif of *combat*: the entire Exodus event is interpreted as a gigantic struggle between the God of Israel and the gods of Egypt, and between Yahweh and Pharaoh. The combat begins and steadily intensifies in the story of the plagues. It reaches its climax in the incidents at the Sea of Reeds, which are presented as a war waged by Yahweh: Yahweh himself enters the lists for Israel and, by overcoming a strong opponent, proves himself the stronger. In winning freedom for his people he reveals his glory and lordship: "The Lord [Yahweh or Kyrios] will reign for ever and ever" (Ex 15:18). This cry of triumph concludes the Song of the Sea of Reeds (Canticle of Moses), which, as Israel's Passover cantata, forms the ending of the Easter Vigil pericope from Exodus. In it the Israelites, who have been led by this saving victory to "believe in the Lord and his servant Moses" (Ex 14:31), proclaim Yahweh as their Lord and King.

We must bear in mind here that the Old Testament already sees this struggle on a deeper level as basically theological in character: Egypt and Pharaoh, its representative, are identified with the primeval, mythical Leviathan or Dragon; Yahweh repeats his chaos-conquering act of creation, and anticipates his eschatological victory, by subduing Leviathan in the Sea of Reeds at the first Passover (Ps 74:12ff.; Is 51:9ff.)

New Testament symbolism, evidently depending here on the Old Testament, likewise uses the Dragon as an image of the forces ranged against God (Rev 12:3ff., and in several other passages). In continuation of this way of thinking, the Fathers regard Pharaoh as a type of the devil and, following Philo, see Egypt as a symbol of the world (in the Johannine sense of this last term). Thus in his Easter homily Melito of Sardis says of Christ "who was led away like a lamb and slaughtered like a sheep":

"He freed us from service to the cosmos as he did from the land of Egypt; he released us from servitude to the devil as he did from the land of Pharaoh. . . . It was he who . . . made the devil mourn as Moses did Pharaoh. . . . It was he who brought us from slavery to freedom, from darkness to light, from death to life, from despotism to an eternal kingdom."

3. The most important point to be made is that the principal terms in our *soteriological vocabulary* have their roots and basis in the Passover-Exodus event. The central concepts of biblical theology—rescue (*ryesthai*), redeem (*lytrousthai*), and save (*sōzein*)—were applied first and foremost to Israel's "Easter" liberation from Egyptian slavery; it is in the Passover that these terms have their true *Sitz im Leben* ("place in life," or vital context). The New Testament uses the same verbs in speaking of salvation; they express (once again by analogy with the Old Testament) the saving action of God and Christ, both as this has already taken place in the paschal act of salvation and as it is still to come at the end of time.

4. It is true that in the Old Testament Passover Yahweh himself is the "redeemer of Israel." But he does nonetheless make use of a *means of salvation* and of a *mediator of salvation*. The means of salvation is the lamb or its blood; the mediator of salvation is Moses, the servant of Yahweh. In the New Testament, Jesus himself is both the true Passover lamb and the new Moses; the early Church took this identification for granted and developed it further. But it too has its roots in Judaism, since in the Jewish tradition about the Exodus, Moses appears as both the servant of Yahweh and the lamb of Yahweh. Correspondingly, in Melito's Easter homily Christ, who is prefigured both by the Passover lamb and by Moses, is at the same time the Servant of God

14

(Second Isaiah) who "like a lamb . . . is led to the slaughter" (Is 53:7).

5. To the christological and soteriological aspects must be added the *sacramental aspect*. I have already spoken of the connection between Passover and the Eucharist. But there is also a connection between Passover and baptism. When Melito of Sardis describes the Passover blood (which the Old Testament interprets as a sign of protection and life) as a "seal" (*sphragis*) and connects it with the "Spirit" (*pneuma*), he is probably thinking of baptism rather than the Eucharist. It was easy to link Passover and baptism in this way inasmuch as in Judaism itself the blood of the Passover lamb was repeatedly treated as parallel with the blood of circumcision. But the real Old Testament prefiguration of baptism at Easter is the crossing of the Sea of Reeds. This type, which plays an important role in the writings of the Fathers,[11] occurs first in Paul, who in turn seems to be making use of a midrash-like explanation of Jewish proselyte baptism: "I want you to know, brethren, that our fathers were all under the cloud, and all passed through the sea, and all were baptized into Moses in the cloud and in the sea" (1 Cor 10:1–2).

THE GIFT OF THE PROMISED LAND

In the view of the early churches baptism assures access to the land flowing with milk and honey. As a sign of this the newly baptized were given a drink of milk and honey that had first been blessed.[12] In addition, the "entrance into rest" (Ps 95:11) is the distant goal to which the pilgrim people of God are always moving as they journey through the wilderness of this world (Heb 4:1–11).

Significantly, the annual celebration of Passover already serves in the Old Testament as a commemoration not only of the Exodus from Egypt but also of the entrance into the Promised Land, which had from the outset been the aim and purpose of the Exodus. The

Passover cantata in Ex 15 and the Alleluia song in Ps 114 as well as Josh 3:14–17 make the crossing of the Jordan, with its resultant entrance into the Promised Land, a parallel to the crossing of the Sea of Reeds. Immediately after the crossing of the Jordan, a connection is established between the Passover custom of eating unleavened bread and the Israelite appropriation of Palestine. For on this occasion, at the time of Passover, the fathers ate for the first time the produce of the Promised Land: "When the people of Israel were encamped in Gilgal they kept the passover on the fourteenth day of the month at evening on the plains of Jericho. And on the morrow after the passover, on that very day, they ate of the produce of the land, unleavened bread and parched grain" (Josh 5:10–11). Since there was no yeast yet available, the bread made from the first fruits of the grain was necessarily unleavened. As a result, the mazzoth eaten at the annual spring festival was a reminder not only of the privations suffered during the enslavement in Egypt and of the haste that marked the departure to freedom, but also of the bestowal of the Promised Land, which was thus celebrated as Yahweh's Easter gift to his people who had been redeemed at Easter.

In the early chapters of the Book of Joshua, it is clearly the cult-legend (that is, the rite and its causal explanation or etiology) of the ancient Israelite spring festival in Nisan/Abib that is being passed on to us. After the Settlement and during the premonarchic period, the twelve tribes assembled annually at Gilgal to celebrate together the feast of unleavened bread, which lasted a full week (probably from sabbath to sabbath). During the festival the takeover of the country was commemorated by a ritual representation of it: a procession across the Jordan (Josh 3:1 to 4:18), and a daily procession around the city of Jericho, which was already a ruin (Josh 6:1–16).

Recent exegetical study has shown the probability that

the feast of unleavened bread which was celebrated at Gilgal was in fact the ancient Israelite covenant festival. In other words: the covenant by which Israel was established as the twelve-tribe people of God and which was later regarded as having been concluded at Sinai (cf. the mention of the twelve memorial pillars both in Ex 24:4 and in Josh 4:1–7, 20–24) was originally celebrated and renewed annually in Gilgal at Easter. On this occasion "the law specifying the privileges of Yahweh" (that is, the "cultic decalogue" in Ex 34:10–26), which gave expression to Yahweh's exclusive claim to possession of his people, was solemnly proclaimed and ratified.[13]

Later on, therefore, when as a result of the Deuteronomic reform, Passover, which by now had been fused with the feast of unleavened bread, became *the* Israelite feast (Deut 16:1–8 and 2 Kings 23:21ff.; cf. 2 Chron 30:1–27 and 35:1–19), this Easter feast was simply regaining the position which (as 2 Kings 23:22 expressly admits) had been proper to it from the beginning. For that matter, even the Priestly Document, which took its literary form during the Exile, emphasizes the point that Passover, although celebrated "in each household" (cf. Ex 12:3, and compare Acts 2:46 and 5:42 where the "breaking of bread" takes place "in their homes" or "at home": *kat'oikon*), is also to be observed (according to Ex 12:3, 6) by "all the congregation of Israel" (that is, by the entire *ekklēsia*!).

The last point is of great interest to us as well: Passover/ Easter, as feast of Israel and the covenant, is the feast of the entire people of God. The same is true of the Eucharist, as we have seen. But it is true also of baptism. For part of the feast of unleavened bread at Gilgal was a ritual not mentioned thus far: circumcision. This rite was to be performed immediately before the feast on any as yet uncircumcised males in order to "roll away the reproach of Egypt from them" (Josh 5:2–9; here again we have an obvious etiology). The sense probably is that in connection with the spring festival at

Gilgal the young men in the age group that had reached its majority that year were accepted, through circumcision, into the people of God as members with full rights and especially as members capable of participating in the public worship.[14] The Priestly Document (Ex 12:47, 48; Num 9:13) also lays strong emphasis on the fact that, on the one hand, only circumcised males are permitted to celebrate the Passover and that, on the other, all circumcised males have an obligation to celebrate it. The same holds for New Testament baptism, which has replaced Old Testament circumcision: as paschal incorporation into the people of God, it is the presupposition of and the initiation into the paschal mystery of the new covenant.[15]

THE BLOOD OF THE COVENANT

In the pericope of the Priestly Document on the so-called covenant with Abraham (Gen 17:1–14), the circumcision which is henceforth performed on the eighth day after birth is called "a sign of the covenant." Through circumcision the Israelite is accepted into the covenant with God and identified as one who belongs to God in a special way. Circumcision requires that (at least a drop of) blood should flow. A special saving power is attributed to this blood of circumcision, as is shown by the early story of Moses being saved by the blood of his son's circumcision when he is threatened with death (Ex 4:24–26). The important thing for us here is the close association which Judaism established between the blood of circumcision and the blood of the Passover lamb: Israel's liberation depends on both the blood of the lamb and the blood of circumcision.[16]

This notion emerges in an especially striking way in the rabbinical exegesis of the Yahweh-Israel allegory in Ezek 16, which is so important for the Jewish theology of Passover. As Yahweh passes by Israel, whom he will later take as his wife, he sees her lying in her blood like a foundling: "I said to you in your blood, 'Live'" (Ezek

16:6). Jewish exegetes interpreted the plural form of "blood" in the Hebrew text as a dual: "in your two bloods," and had Yahweh saying to Israel: "Live by the blood of the Passover lamb, live by the blood of circumcision." Blood gives life, and this is true especially of the blood of Jesus, which is the blood both of the paschal Lamb and of the covenant.

The association here of Passover and covenant (since the blood of circumcision is covenant blood) also emerges from the divine promise which is given at the covenant with Abraham and which in fact reveals the true meaning and content of this "covenant." For, unlike the covenant at Sinai, there is no question here of a reciprocal obligation accepted by Yahweh and Israel, but of a unilateral, self-imposed obligation which Yahweh accepts toward the patriarchs and their descendants.

This unilaterality can be seen with special clarity in the older variant of Gen 17, namely the story of the "covenant between the pieces" in Gen 15. In a nocturnal vision that strongly reminds us of the theophany at Sinai, Yahweh accepts a solemn obligation toward Abraham. The content of this self-imposed obligation is the bestowal of the Promised Land, and, as a condition of this, the liberation from Egyptian slavery. This liberation will in turn lead to a deeper and closer bond between Yahweh and Israel. As a result of this redemptive act, which is motivated by his covenant with their ancestors, Yahweh makes the Israelites his people in order that he may be their God (Ex 6:2–8; but cf., already, Gen 17:7–8). In its present context in the Pentateuch the original promise is fulfilled by the covenant at Sinai (Ex 19 to 24). The covenant is the immediate goal and first fruit of the Exodus which occurs at Passover, and with the Exodus it forms so close a unity that Yahweh can speak of it as "the covenant which I made with their fathers when I took them by the hand to bring them out of the land of Egypt" (Jer 31:32).[17]

The unity of Exodus and covenant and therefore of covenant and Passover is so close that the Book of Wisdom, which in its final part may reproduce a Passover Haggadah used by Alexandrian Jews, can shift the making of the covenant to the night of Passover: "That night was made known beforehand to our fathers, so that they might rejoice in sure knowledge of the oaths in which they trusted. . . . For in secret the holy children of good men offered sacrifices, and with one accord agreed to the divine law,[18] that the saints would share alike in the same things, both blessings and dangers, and already they were singing the praises of the father" (Wis 18:6, 8).

The idea of the covenant being connected with Passover can also be seen in the fact that in the Jewish liturgy the Song of Songs provides the festal scroll for Pesach-Mazzoth; as in the prophets, so here Yahweh is the "bridegroom" who cultivates a relationship with Israel, his "bride," in order to conclude a marriage covenant with her.

As is indicated in the earlier cited midrash on the night of watching (Ex 12:42), the covenant "between the pieces" with Abraham, which is so fundamental for the relationship between Yahweh and Israel, is itself a Passover event to the extent that it was concluded during a Passover night. The assignment to it of a Passover date has a basis in the Old Testament. In Ex 12:40–41 it is said (the allusion is to Gen 15:13–14): "The time that the people of Israel dwelt in Egypt was four hundred and thirty years. And at the end of four hundred and thirty years, on that very day, all the hosts of the Lord went out from the land of Egypt. It was a night of watching. . . ."

The only further point I wish to make here is that in the New Testament too the redemptive Christ-event of Easter is not simply identified with the new covenant that is made in the covenant blood of the new Passover Lamb; in addition, this covenant, like the first Exodus and the first covenant, is the final and truest fruit of the paschal covenant-promise that had been made to the fathers: "Blessed be the Lord God of Israel, for he has visited and redeemed his people, and has raised up a horn of salvation [i.e., a mighty savior] for us . . . that we should be saved from our enemies . . . to perform the mercy promised to our fathers, and to remember his holy covenant, the oath which he swore to our father Abraham. . ." (Lk 1:68–74; cf. also, e.g., 1:54–55).

THE SACRIFICE OF THE BELOVED SON

During the same Passover night in which Yahweh concluded the "covenant between the pieces" with Abraham, there also took place, according to the Jewish theology of Passover, the "Binding of Isaac" (the *Aqedah*), that is, the offering of Isaac in sacrifice by his father Abraham, as narrated in Gen 22:1–19.[19] The oldest witness to this highly significant Passover dating of an event so central in Jewish theology is to be found in the Book of Jubilees, which is undoubtedly a pre-Christian document. Here the sacrifice of Isaac is seen as the origin of the weeklong feast of unleavened bread at Passover time:

"And he [Abraham] celebrated this festival every year, seven days with joy, and he called it the festival of the Lord according to the seven days during which he went [with Isaac to Zion, the mountain of sacrifice] and returned in peace. And accordingly has it been ordained and written on the heavenly tablets regarding Israel and its seed that they should observe this festival seven days [each year] with the joy of festival."[20]

In other words, the sacrifice of Isaac is the real etiology of the Easter festival.

With the Old Testament as its point of departure, Judaism connected with Gen 22 some major themes that are of critical importance for a proper understanding of the New Testament interpretation of Jesus' death and resurrection at Passover.[21] There is, for example, the *theme of the firstborn*. The original point of Gen 22 was to give an etiological explanation of the Israelite cultic practice of sacrificing a male lamb (i.e., a ram; cf. Gen 22:13) in place of the human firstborn, who by rights should have been sacrificed to God. But precisely the same point is being made in the biblical pericope describing the Passover night in Egypt. Yahweh's claim on every firstborn as well as the "redemption" of firstborn sons are explained by the sparing of the Israelite firstborn on that Passover night long ago (Ex 13:1–2, 11–16). Moreover, not only the Passover lamb, which in a sense is sacrificed in place of the Israelite firstborn, but also the unleavened bread is part of this theme, since the unleavened loaves are the first fruits of the new harvest and the new land.[22]

Like Isaac in Gen 22:2, 12, 16 (cf. Heb 11:17), Jesus in the New Testament is the "only" (or "only-begotten": *monogenēs*) and therefore the "beloved" (*agapētos*, which is how the LXX translates the Hebrew *jachîd* in Gen 22) "Son" of the Father (cf. Mk 1:11 and 9:7 par.). Like Abraham, God himself is ready to give his "only Son" (at a Passover!) (Jn 3:16; cf. Mk 12:6 par.). As the one who was sacrificed and then rose from the dead at Passover, Jesus is the "firstborn" and the "first fruits" (1 Cor 15:20; Col 1:18; Rev 1:5). But Christians, who were redeemed by Christ at Passover, can also be legitimately described as "firstborn" (cf. Heb 12:23); they "have been redeemed . . . as first fruits for God" by the blood of the Lamb (Rev 14:4 with 5:9).

For Judaism the (Passover) sacrifice of Isaac was the *prototype of all sacrifice*, so that one scholar has been able to say, with good reason, that Gen 22 "is the key to the doctrine of Atonement or Redemption."[23] All the sacrifices offered in the temple at Jerusalem had their saving value through reference to Isaac, who had long ago been sacrificed on that very spot. For, despite what the text says, the claim was made that Isaac, described as a "lamb," was actually sacrificed, that he shed his blood and died. In this context, emphasis was laid on the fact that at the age of thirty-seven Isaac voluntarily offered himself to God and himself carried the word for the sacrifice to the place of the ritual "like a man carrying his cross on his shoulder." Isaac, as "sufferer" and as "servant of God" (allusion to Is 53), had thus become the prototype of Jewish martyrs and the exemplar of ideal sacrifice[24]; in fact, as I indicated, his was a sacrifice to which a permanent salvific value was attributed. He atoned for the sins of Israel, which owed its election and redemption to the blood of Isaac (in conjunction with the blood of the Passover lamb and the blood of circumcision). For in the blood of the lamb that was used to mark the homes of the Israelites in Egypt, God saw the blood of Isaac, and for his sake spared the Israelites. Not only the Passover blood but also the Passover lamb were to remind God each year of Isaac, "the lamb who was tied to the altar and who presented his neck for the sake of the Lord's name."

The parallel with the New Testamental and Christian understanding of salvation and of the liturgy is striking. In the celebration of the Eucharist the past saving act of Jesus is present to all subsequent generations of Christians and effects their salvation to the extent that it repeatedly reminds not only Christians but God himself of the foundational self-giving of the only-begotten and beloved Son at Passover.

But there is more. The theme of sacrifice is accompanied by the *resurrection motif*. God rescued Isaac from death; inasmuch as Isaac was regarded as having actually died, this rescue meant raising him to new life. The Book of Jubilees considers the real reason for Passover joy to be the fact that long ago Abraham had received back his beloved son, and this "on the third day" (cf. Gen 22:4).[25] Also relevant here is the conviction that the sacrifice of Isaac was not only the prototype but also the cause of the resurrection of the dead that is to be expected at the end of time: "In view of the merits of

Isaac, who himself was sacrificed on the altar, God will some day raise the dead to life."

That the resurrection of the dead was actually linked to Passover is also clear from the fact that Ezekiel's vision of the dead bones which are raised to new life (Ezek 37:1–14, one of the classical readings for the Christian Easter Vigil) was at an early date used as the reading from the prophets on the sabbath of Mazzoth-week in the synagogal liturgy. What Isaac was for the Jews, Jesus is for Christians: the One who was raised from the dead on Easter and is the cause of our joy and resurrection.

THE OLD AND THE NEW CREATIONS

After all that has been said, the reason why Gen 22 is read in the Christian liturgy of the Easter Vigil should be clear. But why is Gen 1 used as the first reading? Because the creation of the world is also a Passover or Easter event, and in fact the first of all Passover events. In striking agreement with the Prologue of John, the midrash on the four great Passover nights says: "The first night: when the Lord was revealed over the world to create it. The world was without form and void and darkness was spread over the face of the abyss (Gen 1:2) and the Word of the Lord was the Light, and it shone."

In the pre-Christian Book of Jubilees, the creation of the world is already dated as occurring in the Passover month of Nisan, while for Philo of Alexandria this same spring month of Nisan, together with the spring equinox, which coincides with Passover at the middle of the month, is an image of the beginning of all things. Consequently the Passover feast in spring serves as a "commemoration of the origin of the world." According to Philo, God's very being entails the necessity of the world being created in the spring of the year because his perfection requires that he have called the universe into existence amid the flowering beauty of spring's glory. From this kind of reasoning, which is also found to some extent in Palestinian Judaism, it follows that the moon was created at the full and that the fourth day of the six days of creation should be the same as the day of the full moon and should therefore come at mid-month and thus at the date of Passover.

All this deserves mention because in the New Testament, Christians are described as a "new creation" (2 Cor 5:17; Gal 5:17) on account of their rebirth that results from Christ's paschal work of redemption, and because later on the Church Fathers liked to make use of the spring motif in their mystagogical sermons during the Easter season. Their theme was that God who created the world as a wonderful place has even more wonderfully renewed it, and the annual awakening of nature to new life is richly symbolic of this spiritual renewal.[26]

Like the creation of the world, the creation of human beings evidently occurred at Passover time; on the basis of the calculations indicated a moment ago, this creation fell specifically on the Friday after the spring full moon.[27] The Book of Jubilees (2:14; 3:8) places the creation of Eve from Adam's side on the same day on which Adam himself was given life. This point is worth noting because according to the gospel of John (cf. 19:34), it was on the same date and weekday of Passover that Jesus died on the cross and his side was opened; Christian writers were soon saying that the blood and water which flowed from the opened side and to which they gave a sacramental interpretation also symbolized the creation of the Church as a new Eve from the side of the new Adam (cf. 1 Cor 15:22, 45).

The correspondence (in time as well as in content) between creation and redemption, between the old and the new creations, and between the old and the new Adams, represents a legitimate further development of a motif already present in the Old Testament. For in the Old Testament there already exists a correspondence, which evidently is deliberately intended, between God's action in creating the world and his action at the

Sea of Reeds when he climaxes the events of Passover. In both cases God struggles victoriously with the "dragon," which represents in the first case the chaotic primordial waters that precede the ordered universe (e.g., Ps 89:10ff.), and in the second, Egypt and Pharaoh as Israel's archetypal enemy (e.g., Ps 74:12ff.). It has therefore been said with good reason that "as the world was created out of water, so Israel as a historical people was rescued from being catastrophically overwhelmed in water and was formed into a people" (Sigmund Mowinckel).

A third and final struggle between God and the "dragon" will lead to the definitive annihilation of the latter and thus to the eschatological time of salvation (cf. Is 27:1; Rev 12:7ff.). Thus the creation of the world, the redemption, and the final salvation are interrelated as three paschal events at the beginning, middle, and end of time. The one God who acts paschally through his "word" is at once creator of the world (Gen 1:1), "creator of Israel" (Is 43:1, 15), and creator of "new heavens and a new earth" (Is 65:17; Rev 21:1).

THE COMING OF THE MESSIAH
This brings us to the final Passover event. Just as the creation of the world and the redemption of Israel took place on a Passover, so the Jews of the time of Jesus and the apostles expected that eschatological salvation, involving the definitive redemption of Israel and the renewal of the world, would come on a Passover. The Old Testament already sees the coming final salvation as analogous with the liberation of Israel from Egyptian slavery.

We need think here only of Second Isaiah. During the Exile he foresaw and described salvation as a new Exodus, but on the eschatological plane. Correspondingly, the verbs for salvation: rescue, redeem, save, which originated in the soteriology of Passover-Exodus, were transferred to the final intervention of

26

Yahweh that was still to come. From this it was but a small step to assigning a Passover date to the future decisive Passover action of God. This step was in fact taken in the pre-Christian period as can be seen from the Septuagint translation of Jer 31(38):8. Here, shortly before the passage on the promised new covenant, God says of the Israelites who are dispersed in exile and are to be brought together from the four corners of the earth: "I will gather them from the ends of the earth on the feast of Passover."

Final salvation is linked to the coming of the Messiah. At the beginning of the Christian era this coming was expected to occur at a Passover, as is clear from, among other sources, the remarks of the Jewish historian, Flavius Josephus, who says that at the feast of Passover political uprisings were constantly occurring among the crowds of pilgrims due to their intense expectation of the Messiah's coming at Passover. Against this background the reaction to the entrance of Jesus into Jerusalem just before Passover becomes intelligible: "Hosanna [to the son of David]! Blessed is he who comes in the name of the Lord [Ps 118:25–26]! Blessed is the kingdom of our father David that is coming! Hosanna in the highest!" (Mk 11:9–10; cf. Mt 21:9; Lk 19:38; Jn 12:13–14). The acclamation with which the crowd greets and accompanies Jesus is from Ps 118; it was also recited at the slaughter of the Passover lambs and at the Passover meal (as one of the Hallel psalms), and was at that time generally given a messianic interpretation.[28]

Admittedly, messianic expectations at the beginning of the Christian era were extremely varied. This is clear, for example, from the midrash on the four Passover nights:

"The fourth night: When the world reaches its end to be redeemed: the yokes of iron shall be broken and the generations of wickedness shall be blotted out; and

Moses will go up from the desert and the king Messiah from on high. One will lead at the head of ⟨a cloud or:⟩ the flock and the other will lead at the head of ⟨a cloud or:⟩ the flock and his Word will lead between the two of them, and . . . they will proceed together."

Here three or even four savior figures are mentioned. *Moses* will return and, as the resurrection of the dead implies, will bring with him the Israelites who died during the sojourn in the wilderness. The *Messiah* will come, together with the exiles who have been gathered from the four winds; he will come "from on high," [29] that is, as the mention of the "cloud" suggests,[30] he will come as the heavenly *Son of Man*. These figures will be accompanied by the personified *Word of God* who was active as "the Light" at the creation of the world and, as the Passover Haggadah in Wis 18:14–15 reports, also manifested himself at the Passover in Egypt as executor of God's command: "While gentle silence enveloped all things, and night in its swift course was now half gone, thy all-powerful word leaped from heaven, from the royal throne, into the midst of the land that was doomed, a stern warrior . . ." (cf. also Rev 19:11ff.).

In the New Testament—and this is the properly new element in the "New" Testament—one and the same Jesus of Nazareth combines all these figures in himself. He is the eschatological prophet and servant of God and therefore the Moses whose return was expected; the royal Messiah from the House of David; the Word of God made flesh—and at the same time the lamb who was sacrificed on a Passover as the new paschal victim by whose blood we are redeemed and have life.

But the expectation of Christ's return at a Passover was far from disappearing in the early Church. The Jesus who was exalted at Passover as "Lord and Christ" (Acts 2:36) was also expected to return on a Passover. For when Christians are told in the New Testament to wait with "loins girded" and keep watch (Lk 12:35; cf. 1 Pet

1:13; Eph 6:14), because the Lord will come "at midnight" as a "bridegroom" (Mt 25:6), they are being put
in mind of Passover night, as the verbatim citations
show (Ex 12:11 and 12:29; Wis 18:14).

This expectation that the end would come on Passover
showed up in the early Church, and not only in Quartodeciman circles. It also exerted an important influence
on the theology of the Easter Vigil in the western
Church. Here, the Pasch "is the night which we celebrate with a nocturnal vigil on account of the parousia of
our King and God. Its content is twofold: during this
night he will later acquire lordship over the world."[32]
And even two hundred years later Jerome is able to
write:

"There is a Jewish tradition that Christ will come at
midnight, after the manner of the time in Egypt when,
as the Passover was being celebrated, the destroyer
came and the Lord passed over the tents and the doorposts of our foreheads were consecrated by the blood of
the lamb. This, I think, is why the practice has been
retained as an apostolic tradition that during the Easter
Vigil the crowds who await the coming of Christ are not
to be dismissed before midnight. Once this hour has
passed, all celebrate the feastday with renewed confidence."[33]

The Old Testamental and Jewish Passover is truly the
root of our Easter celebration. The more fully we retain
our link with this root (or rediscover it), the better we
will be able to understand our own paschal mystery and
make it intelligible to others, and the more fully we will
be able to join wholeheartedly in the Easter praise that
finds expression in our Christian *Exsultet*:

"This is the night when first you saved *our* fathers;
you freed the people of Israel from their slavery
and led them dry-shod through the sea.

"This is the night when the pillar of fire
destroyed the darkness of sin!

"This is the night when Christians everywhere,
 washed clean of sin
 and freed from all defilement,
 are restored to grace and grow together in holiness.

"This is the night when Jesus Christ
 broke the chains of death
 and rose triumphant from the grave. . . .

"Of this night scripture says:
 'The night will be as clear as day:
 it will become my light, my joy.'

"The power of this holy night
 dispels all evil, washes guilt away,
 restores lost innocence, brings mourners joy;
 it casts out hatred, brings us peace, and humbles
     earthly pride.

"Night truly blessed. . . ."

NOTES

1. Text and commentary in J. Blank, *Meliton von Sardes: Vom
Pascha. Die älteste christliche Osterpredigt* (Sophia 3; Freiburg,
West Germany, 1963). (There is also an edition with text,
French translation, and commentary: Othmar Perler, *Meliton
de Sardes: Sur la Pâque* [Sources chrétiennes 123; Paris, 1966].)
On the early Christian development of the feast of Easter, cf.
also W. Huber, *Passa und Ostern. Untersuchungen zur Osterfeier der alten Kirche* (BZNW 35; Berlin, 1969); contains a bib-
liography.

2. While the Jews were eating their Passover meal, the Quar-
todecimans fasted. This early Christian "Good Friday fast,"
out of which the pre-Easter season of fasting gradually developed, may be connected with the words of Jesus in Mk 2:20
par.: "The days will come, when the bridegroom is taken
away from them, and then they [the disciples of Jesus] will
fast in that day."

3. Thus, recently, R. Pesch, *Das Markusevangelium* 2 (Herder's
Theologischer Kommentar zum Neuen Testament II/2; Freiburg,

West Germany, 1977), pp. 323–28. Cf. idem, *Wie Jesus das Abendmahl hielt* (Freiburg, West Germany, 1977). The standard work is still Joachim Jeremias, *The Eucharistic Words of Jesus*, trans. N. Perrin (London, 1966).

4. The following more recent monographs deal with the historical development of the Israelite spring festival: J.B. Segal, *The Hebrew Passover from the Earliest Times to A.D. 70* (London, 1963); P. Laaf, *Das Pascha-Feier Israels (Bonner Biblische Beiträge* 36; Bonn, 1970); H. Haag, *Vom alten zum neuen Pascha (Stuttgarter Biblische Schriften* 49; Stuttgart, 1971); R. Schmitt, *Exodus und Pascha. Ihre Zusammenhang im Alten Testament (Orbis biblicus et orientalis* 7 Freiburg-Sch.—Göttinger, West Germany; 1975); J. Henninger, *Les fêtes du printemps chez les sémites et la Pâque israélite* (Etudes bibliques; Paris, 1975).

5. Details and sources for the following discussion are given in N. Füglister, *Die Heilsbedeutung des Pascha (Studien zum Alten und Neuen Testament* 8; Munich, 1963); cf. idem, "Die Heilsbedeutung des Pascha im alten Bund," *Lebendiges Zeugnis*, no. 3 (1965), pp. 7–29; idem, "Passover," *Sacramentum mundi* 4:352–57.

6. The Mishnah, Treatise Pesahim 10, 5, in H. Danby (ed.), *The Mishnah* (Oxford, 1933), p. 151.

7. On the expiatory power of the sacrificial blood, cf. N. Füglister, *Die Heilsbedeutung des Pascha*, pp. 77–105; idem, "Sühne durch Blut. Zur Bedeutung von Leviticus 17, 11," in G. Braulik (ed.), *Studien zum Pentateuch. Festschrift für A. Kornfeld* (Vienna, 1977), pp. 143–64.

8. There is a detailed discussion of this text and its implications in R. Le Déaut, *La nuit pascale. Essai sur la signification de la Pâque juive à partir du Targum d'Exode XII 42 (Analecta Biblica* 22; Rome, 1963). The English translation here is by M. McNamara in A. Diez Macho, *Ms Neophyti 1 2. Exodo* (Madrid—Barcelona, 1970), pp. 441–42. [The italics are in McNamara's translation; I have added the scripture references and the words in ⟨ ⟩ from Füglister's German version.—Tr.]

9. It is evident that this cannot be brought up for discussion for the first time during the Easter Vigil itself. The introduction of the texts and themes must be undertaken during the preceding Lent in sermons, religious instruction, adult educa-

tion courses, and Bible study groups. Lent would then become what Vatican II meant it to be: an annual catechumenate that will repeatedly and more fully introduce Christians into the paschal mystery.

10. Cf. N. Füglister, "Feier des Lebens. Ostern als Fest der Auferstechung vom Alten Testament her gesehen," in Th. Bogler (ed.), *Ostern—Fest der Auferstehung heute* (Liturgie und Mönchtum 42; Maria Laach, 1968), pp. 21–27.

11. Cf. J. Daniélou, *From Shadows to Reality. Studies in the Biblical Typology of the Fathers*, trans. W. Hibberd (Westminster, Md., 1960), pp. 175–201; idem, *The Bible and the Liturgy* (Notre Dame, Ind., 1956), pp. 86–98.

12. Cf. 1 Pet 2:2 and the discussion in K. H. Schelkle, *Die Petrusbriefe* (Herder's *Theologischer Kommentar zum Neuen Testament* XIII/2; Freiburg, West Germany, 1964²), pp. 55–56.

13. Cf. E. Otto, *Das Mazzotfest in Gilgal (Beiträge zur Wissenschaft vom Alten und Neuen Testament* VI/7; Stuttgart, 1975), and J. Halbe, *Das Privilegrecht Jahwes Ex 34, 10–26* (*Forschungen zur Religion und Literatur des Alten und Neuen Testaments* 114; Göttingen, West Germany, 1975).

14. Cf. Ex 24:5. At Sinai the covenant sacrifice was offered by "young men [perhaps just initiated] of the people of Israel"[!]

15. On the connection between circumcision and baptism (cf. Col 2:11; Phil 3:3), cf. J. Daniélou, "Circoncision et baptême," in *Theologie in Geschichte und Gegenwart. Festschrift für Michael Schmaus* (Munich, 1957), pp. 755–76.

16. Cf. also Zech 9:11: "Because of the blood of my covenant with you, I will set your captives free from the waterless pit." In Judaism this text was interpreted as referring not only to the blood of the Sinai covenant but also to the covenant blood shed at circumcision and at Passover.

17. The Sinai covenant, which Ex 19:1 says was concluded in the third month after leaving Egypt, was connected with Pentecost in late, post-Old Testament Judaism. But the feast of Pentecost was already closely linked to the feast of unleavened bread in the Old Testament itself; Pentecost marked the end of the fifty-day harvest season that began with the offering of the first fruits on the day after the sabbath of unleavened bread; it could therefore be designated in Judaism as "conclusion (feast

of)." In the New Testament and early Christianity the feast of Pentecost (which Acts describes in ways reminiscent of the Sinai event) is likewise the conclusion of the Easter event and the Easter season.

18. "To bind oneself to the Law of God" (*diatithesthai*) is a technical term in biblical Greek for concluding a covenant (or agreement, treaty = *diathēkē*) and especially the Sinai covenant.

19. In addition, the birth of Isaac and the "annunciation" of it exactly a year before (cf. Gen 18:1–15) are dated on the 15th of Nisan. This entry on the scene of the son of the promise at Passover is represented in the Old Testament as a marvel wrought by God. Judaism went even further (cf. Philo of Alexandria and Pseudo-Philo): God himself forms Isaac in Sarah's "virginal" womb in order that he, God, may be a father to this boy in a very special way. There is here a notable parallel to the New Testament account of the conception of Jesus, which the early Church writers (e.g., Tertullian) likewise connected with the date of Easter.

20. 18:18–19; trans. in R.H. Charles (ed.), *The Apocrypha and Pseudepigrapha of the Old Testament* 2 (Oxford, 1913), p. 40. Cf. also Jubilees 17:15, 18:3.

21. Details in Füglister, *Die Heilsbedeutung des Pascha*, pp. 210–19. In addition to Le Déaut, *La nuit pascale*, pp. 133–212, cf. G. Vermès, *Scripture and Tradition in Judaism* (Leiden, 1973²), pp. 193–227, and D. Lerch, *Isaaks Opferung christlich gedeutet (Beiträge zur historischen Theologie* 12; Tübingen, West Germany, 1950). In connection with some of the following statements about Isaac the question arises, of course, as to whether they may not owe their origin to polemics between Jews and Christians. That is, the suspicion arises that the Jews may have subsequently attributed to "their" Isaac what the Christians were claiming about "their" Jesus.

22. Cf. what was said earlier about Jos 5. In addition, during the covenant festival at Passover in Gilgal postulated here, there was an annual dedication of the firstborn in response to Ex 34:18–20: "Seven days you shall eat unleavened bread, as I commanded you, at the time appointed in the month Abib; for in the month of Abib you came out from Egypt. All that opens the womb is mine. . . . All the firstborn of your sons you shall redeem. And none shall appear before me empty."

33

23. Vermès, op. cit., p. 193.

24. I must mention here that the killing of Abel by Cain (Gen 4:3–16) and the liberation from the fiery furnace of the three young men who offered themselves as a sacrifice for the people (Dan 3:21–50) were also regarded as Passover events. Dan 3:1–24 used to be the twelfth reading of the Christian Easter Vigil, and in the New Testament the blood of Abel is already associated with the blood of Christ "that speaks more graciously than the blood of Abel" (Heb 12:24). In Melito's Easter homily the "mystery of the Lord" is not simply regarded as prefigured in Abel and Isaac; rather, Christ himself, "the Passover sacrifice of our salvation," suffered in Abel and Isaac: "It is he who was slain in Abel, bound in Isaac, sold in Joseph, exposed in Moses, persecuted in David, scorned in the prophets."

25. Jubilees 18:3. This interpretation, in which Isaac is restored to life, is echoed in the New Testament: "By faith Abraham, when he was tested, offered up Isaac, and he who had received the promises was ready to offer up his own son. . . . He considered that God was about to raise men even from the dead; hence he did receive him back and this was a symbol" (Heb 11:17–18; cf. Rom 14:17–21).

26. Cf., among others, H. Rahner, "Österliche Frühlingslyrik bei Kyrillos von Alexandreia," in B. Fischer and J. Wagner (eds.), *Paschatis Solemnia. Studien zur Osterfeier und Osterfrömmigkeit* (Freiburg, West Germany, 1959), pp. 68–75, and A. Kirchgässner, "Ostern das christliche Neujahrsfest," ibid., pp. 49–56.

27. In connection with the creation of the world, Melito's homily likewise speaks of "formation of man by the Word." He goes on to speak of sin and the fall.

28. The expectation of the Messiah also finds expression in the prayers and blessings of the liturgy for the Passover meal.

29. Or, according to a variant, "from Rome." The idea that the Messiah lives hidden near the gates of Rome also occurs elsewhere in rabbinical literature.

30. The Aramaic expression is ambiguous; it can mean either "cloud" or "flock."

31. Interestingly enough, the Easter homily of Melito of Sardis gives no basis for the idea of a proximate coming of Christ at Easter. Instead there is the cultic manifestation of the risen Lord in the midst of the worshiping community; in adopting this "realized eschatology," Melito is in the tradition of the gospel of John.

32. Lactantius, *Divinae institutiones* VII, 19, 3 (*Patrologia Latina* 6:797). Cf., at an earlier date, Tertullian, *De baptismo* 19 (*Corpus Scriptorum Ecclesiasticorum Latinorum* 20:217): Christ will return *"in Pascha"*; Tertullian refers here to Jer 31(38):8, which has "on the feast of Passover" in the Septuagint.

33. *In evangelium Matthaei* 25, 6 (*Patrologia Latina* 26:192). The final sentence of the passage shows that the longing expectation of Christ's return, as reflected in the New Testament ("Come, Lord Jesus!"), is already beginning to yield place to fear of the judgment; the *Maranatha* of the early Church is turning into the *Dies irae* of the Middle Ages.

Content and Form of the Easter Vigil

A liturgy is not simply a series of songs, readings, and prayers that might just as well have been placed in a different order. On the contrary, every liturgy has a basic structure, a law governing its construction, in accordance with which the parts combine to form a whole. If, then, we want to celebrate the Easter Vigil properly with our communities, we must recognize and understand the law of its structure. Only then will we be able to lay the proper emphasis on the individual parts and give a vital form to the whole.

THE GOAL AND FOCAL POINT OF THE EASTER VIGIL IS THE EUCHARIST ON THE THRESHOLD OF EASTER DAY
The Church celebrates the Lord's resurrection by means of the Eucharist. Such a practice reflects the experience of the apostles themselves. The latter, after all, were not eyewitnesses to the resurrection as an event (not even the guards at the tomb were eyewitnesses in this sense); rather they bear witness to us that the Lord appeared to them after his resurrection and that they were privileged to eat and drink with him.

Thus Peter gives the following testimony to the pagan centurion Cornelius: "And we are witnesses to all that he did both in the country of the Jews and in Jerusalem. They put him to death by hanging him on a tree; but God raised him on the third day and made him manifest; not to all the people but to us who were chosen by God as witnesses, who ate and drank with him after he rose from the dead" (Acts 10:39–41).

The disciples bear a similar witness at Emmaus, as do the Twelve in the upper room (Lk 24:31, 41–43); such too is the experience of the disciples at the Sea of Gennesaret (Jn 21:12). In like manner the Church experiences and bears witness down the centuries to the fact that the Lord died on the cross and rose from the dead for our salvation. An Easter celebration that reflects this kind of experience is attested as early as the middle of the second century; Jerome has preserved for us some fragments of the *Gospel of the Hebrews*, and there we read:

"James had sworn that he would not eat bread from that hour in which he had drunk the cup of the Lord until he should see him risen among them from that sleep. And shortly thereafter the Lord said: Bring a table and bread! And immediately it is added: he took the bread, blessed it and brake it and gave it to James the Just and said to him: My brother, eat thy bread, for the Son of man is risen from among them that sleep."[1]

Today the Lord still says to his followers: Take and eat, come and eat, for the Son of man has risen from the dead. Easter occurs again today whenever Christ comes to us as victor and gives us a share in his sacrifice and his triumph. The Easter Eucharist is the original and principal Eucharist of the entire year, and even now every Christian is obliged to receive communion during the Easter season (*in Paschate*). All reflection on and planning for the Easter Vigil celebration must therefore start from the principle that the Eucharist on the threshold of Easter day is the goal and focal point of the entire Vigil celebration.

As the passage about James makes clear, this Eucharist was understood from the beginning as the "breaking of the fast": for as long as the bridegroom is taken away from them, the wedding guests will fast; when they have the bridegroom with them (once again), they will cease to fast (Mk 2:19–20). For this reason, the Easter celebration includes not only the Easter Eucharist but also the days and hours during which Christ is taken from the community. During this time they are unable to celebrate the joyous Easter wedding feast. Instead, they wait, full of longing, for the Lord to return as conqueror and to invite the fasting community to his table for the victory banquet of the Eucharist.

The Easter celebration thus embraces both cross and resurrection. It is "a passover, that is, a passage" (*Pascha, id est transitus*), a passage from death to life, a crossing of the Red Sea to our homeland. Thus the Easter Eucharist again becomes the hinge and focal point of the entire celebration.

IN LONGING EXPECTATION OF THE EASTER EUCHARIST THE CHURCH WATCHES AND PRAYS DURING THE EASTER VIGIL

The Old Testament people of God had likewise not slept during this night: "On that very day, all the hosts of the Lord went out from the land of Egypt. It was a night of watching by the Lord, to bring them out of the land of Egypt; so this same night is a night of watching kept to the Lord by all the people of Israel throughout their generations" (Ex 12:41–42). And just as ever since the days in Egypt Israel has spent this night waiting for the coming of the Savior and Messiah, so during this same night Christendom waits for the return of the Lord and Redeemer. Christians know that they are invited to his table when he comes, whether that coming be in the glory of the Parousia or in the hiddenness of the Eucharist.

During this night of waiting the Church tries to observe that to which the Lord exhorts her in the parable:

"Let your loins be girded and your lamps burning, and be like men who are waiting for their master to come home from the marriage feast, so that they may open to him at once when he comes and knocks. Blessed are those servants whom the master finds awake when he comes; truly, I say to you, he will gird himself and have them sit at table, and he will come and serve them. If he comes in the second watch, or in the third, and finds them so, blessed are those servants!" (Lk 12:35–38).

During this night of waiting for her Lord, the Church tries to do as the prudent virgins did in the parable: She stands ready, with lighted lamps, in order to enter the banquet hall with the Lord when he comes for the wedding feast (Mt 25:1–13). Therefore the community lights the lamps for the Easter Vigil and in their light sits and listens to the great deeds which God did for their fathers; for only thus can the Church persevere through the tribulation of our time and, even in a world such as ours, wait in faith for the Lord's coming.

The nucleus of the nocturnal vigil, the backbone of the Easter night celebration, is therefore the liturgy of the word. Unfortunately, this liturgy is often treated like a stepmother; in the consciousness of priests and communities it is often obscured by the glow of the *Exsultet* and the splendor of baptism and the Eucharist. And yet without this watchful praying and listening, the Eucharist loses its character as goal; without this patient absorption in the word of God, the *lucernarium*, or festive lighting of the lamps, is overemphasized and is misinterpreted as being already part of the celebration of the resurrection. As a result, the entire celebration becomes top-heavy.

If the night vigil is to develop in due order, enough time must be allowed for the liturgy of the word; this liturgy must also have a sufficiently emphatic form. The important thing here, however, is less the number of readings chosen than the care with which they are chosen and proclaimed, and with which the community is brought to a right frame of mind. What matters even more is the intensity with which prayer springs from reading and song. In practice, people nowadays tend to speak only of readings when in fact they mean the entire liturgy of the word. But the aim of a liturgy of the word is not simply the hearing of a pericope; it is rather the interior reception and appropriation of the message, the verbalized consent of the community to it in the reponsorial psalm, and the prayer to which everything is meant to lead. The best check on the "success" of the liturgy of the word (if it be legitimate to use a term like "success" in the realm of worship) is and remains the atmosphere of prayer to which it gives rise in the congregation.

In explaining the chosen readings we should then take into account the responsorial psalm of the community and, even more, the concluding prayer which is meant to sum up and express the thoughts and feelings that have come alive in the hearts of the congregation. But this flowering within the community liturgy will not take place without a corresponding intense preparation on the part of priest, reader, and cantor.

As Easter morning draws near, the deacon (priest) enters the watching and praying community and proclaims the message of the apostles: The Lord is truly risen! In these words from the gospel the cry echoes: Up! The Bridegroom is coming! At this proclamation Christ enters into the midst of his watching community and invites them to celebrate the victory banquet with him. After the final reading from the Old Testament, the morning song of Easter, the Gloria, is sung as a greeting to the Lord; at this point the candles on the altar are lit and the bells ring out for the feast. During the procession to the ambo or lectern, the Alleluia, silent during Lent, is heard once again. The proclamation of the Easter gospel is the first climax of the night vigil, and everything should be done to let the community experience this climax by giving the proclamation a duly festive form.

THE EXSULTET AND THE REST OF THE LUCERNARIUM ARE NOT THE CLIMAX OF THE EASTER CELEBRATION BUT THE BEGINNING OF THE NOCTURNAL VIGIL

Many people would call the Exsultet the first climax of the Easter Vigil celebration. But what has been said thus far should have made it clear how thoroughly we would misunderstand the service of light, which opens the celebration, if we were to interpret it as a climax and as a proclamation of the resurrection. As a matter of fact, the lighting of lamps, or lucernarium, is the natural beginning of any nocturnal vigil. Of course, given the length and importance of the Easter Vigil, this normal opening ritual is extensively developed. In fact, it combines a number of customs associated with the lighting of the lamps.

The first custom is simply the lighting of a fire and the taking of light from this and passing it on. Even if this were done in complete silence, it would be an impressive and eloquent ceremony: the fire which God allows to be struck from the stone so that amid the darkness of night we may not lack for warmth and light; the passing from neighbor to neighbor of the light that eventually forms a chain of light binding all together in love.

A second ritual is the greeting of the light, a ceremony which was taken for granted each evening in antiquity and still occurs daily at the beginning of Vespers in a number of Christian liturgies. When the deacon brings the light into the community and announces Christ's presence as the Light that never fades, he is greeted by the thankful cry: "Thanks be to God!" This custom naturally affects us more deeply on this night than on others, for it speaks directly of Christ as the risen Lord who is now the Light shining in the world's darkness. But it does not speak only of this, despite a fairly common misunderstanding. In fact, in the paschal candle the Church sees also, and even more, a symbol of the radiant pillar of fire and cloud that went before the people on their journey across the Red Sea to their homeland. In a comparable way, the congregation advances behind the cloud of incense and the lit candle into their homeland, the house of God.

A third custom is the praise of the light, which the deacon says or sings. The *praeconium paschale*, or Easter hymn of praise, is not an Easter homily, but simply a hymn of praise and petition pronounced over the candle that is to burn and give light to the community during the entire nocturnal vigil, until the morning star finally arises. The petition speaks quite simply of the morning star in the natural world which tells that Easter day has come but which also symbolizes the true "Morning Star which never sets." The hymn of praise covers the entire content of the Easter Vigil, from the night of the Passover lamb in Egypt via the night at the Sea of Reeds and the night of baptism in which the redeemer has saved us, down to the final night when Christ returns as the Morning Star that ushers in our everlasting day. The community celebrates this night by reading of God's mercy in the scriptures, singing of it, and calling upon the Lord to come.

Once this structure is understood, one will not be tempted to devote too much time to this opening rite of the Vigil but will treat it in a simple and straightforward way as what it is meant to be: the lighting of the lamps that will fill the night with light for us.

BAPTISM DURING THE EASTER VIGIL JOINS THE CANDIDATES TO THE CONGREGATION SO THAT ALL TOGETHER MAY CELEBRATE THE VICTORY BANQUET OF EASTER

It is not really self-evident that baptism should be administered during the Easter Vigil. It did, of course, become associated with Easter at a very early date. Tertullian, for example, already speaks of the Easter season (down to Pentecost) as the time especially appropriate for baptism. On the other hand, the Easter Vigil moves without a break from the proclamation of the Easter message to the Eucharist, the victorious sacrifice of the Lord at the altar. The practice of conferring baptism during the Easter Vigil, which gradually became a set custom in the fourth century, seems to have originated in the desire to bring all members of the community together for this decisive, principal, and original Eucharist of the entire year; to this end it was necessary to incorporate all suitable candidates into the Church through baptism and confirmation before this Eucharist was celebrated during the Vigil. This seems clear from the fact that most in the congregation were unable to be onlookers at the baptism (which was usually conferred in the baptistery, a separate room or building) but only saw the newly baptized join the congregation wearing their white garments and carrying their lighted candles. The growth of the Church and the maternal womb of the Church are thus also the motifs (less familiar to us today) that keep recurring in the baptismal texts of the Easter Vigil.

In our concrete situation infant baptism is the usual thing, and it is therefore best to organize the procession of parents, godparents, and candidates with this in mind. As the litany is being recited, the group involved in the baptism is led from the sacristy to the altar or other place of baptism; meanwhile, in the sight and hearing of all, the font is filled with water. While the candidates are gathering around the font, the priest sings the praises of God over the water; this will help the congregation to a better understanding of the mystery of baptism in water and the Holy Spirit. Then come the baptismal profession of faith, the administration of baptism, and confirmation, or in the case of infants, the anointing of the crown of the head.

We can see clearly here that the real purpose of the "consecration of the baptismal water" is frustrated if baptism is not actually administered during the Easter Vigil. It is understandable, of course, that one or another family should be unable to attend the Vigil and should therefore celebrate the baptism of their child later on with water prepared during the Vigil. What is not understandable is that the water should be blessed during the Easter Vigil if no candidates at all are to be presented for baptism on this occasion. Clerical circles continue to speak erroneously of a "blessing of baptismal water" during the Easter Vigil, without reflecting that such a blessing is in preparation for a baptism and for that alone.

When a baptism is actually celebrated during the Easter Vigil, it is natural for the gathered community to associate itself with the newly baptized in the acceptance of a common responsibility and renew its own baptismal promises. This renewal of baptismal promises should therefore be done in the visible presence of the newly baptized and their families.

The Easter Vigil marks the completion, the final step in the initiation of the newly baptized. Even in the case of children who are not yet admitted to communion, this aspect of the Eucharist should nonetheless be given visible expression. In many cases the infants can remain present during the Mass; in any event, the godparents and some members of the families should have places of honor during the celebration of the Eucharist. The candles of the newly baptized should also be placed in sight on the altar or at the places of honor and kept burning during Mass.

The celebration of Easter cannot be limited to the church building. It has traditionally been continued in the family at breakfast on Easter morning or even, as far as possible, in a larger social gathering of the community. In this connection use may be made of the ancient custom of blessing food. The original point of this was to bless those foods that had been set aside during Lent and now were to be enjoyed again for the first time on Easter. But even though the practice of fasting has been relaxed or has even completely disappeared, the blessing of various foods retains a paschal significance. It helps us realize that even in the family home we sit at the table of God.

Just as it used to be customary to take Easter water home or bring it to the cemetery, so now the custom of carrying the Easter light home and to the cemetery is spreading, thus bringing new light and a new hope into the situations of everyday life.

Finally, pastors should seriously reflect that the Easter celebration, like any other liturgical celebration, is not an end in itself. It takes place not for its own sake but in order to help us to conduct the whole of life in the spirit and name of Christ. For only when our life in its entirety, and not just a few hours of it, belongs to God is he glorified and we receive the gift of life.

NOTE

1. Cited in Jerome, *De viris illustribus* 2 (*Patrologia Latina* 23) and translated in E. Hennecke and W. Schneemelcher (eds.), *New Testament Apocrypha* 1, trans. directed by R. McL. Wilson (Philadelphia, 1963), p. 165.

II. Homiletic Development

Importance and Overview

The Easter Vigil is the "mother of all vigils," a "night of watching for the Lord." The liturgy of the word is therefore an essential part of the celebration: the readings proclaim what the Lord has done for his people, while in the songs and prayers we praise him for it.

The Easter Vigil celebration itself allows little time for an extended explanation of the readings; on the other hand, Lent is meant as a preparation for Easter. It is very important, therefore, that the themes of the Vigil be developed during Lent. This is to be done in connection with the readings for the Sundays of Lent.

The homiletic explanation of the Easter Vigil during Lent will ensure that the celebration does not come upon us as an isolated climactic moment, the contents of which we are unable to absorb. Instead, during Lent (and the same holds analogously for the Easter season) the various aspects of the annual feast of Easter are opened up for us. In this way the faithful will become increasingly familiar with the liturgy of the Easter Vigil and will be able to celebrate it in a wholehearted and profitable way.

The homilies offered here are connected with the following Sundays of Lent:

YEAR A
Third Sunday of Lent: Gospel, Jn 4:5–42 (Jesus at the well of Jacob)

Fourth Sunday of Lent: Gospel, Jn 9:1–41 (Healing of the man born blind)

Fifth Sunday of Lent: Gospel, Jn 11:1–45 (Christ the resurrection and the life)

YEAR B

Second Sunday of Lent: first reading, Gen 22:1–2, 9a, 10–13, 15–18 (The sacrifice offered by Abraham our father)

Fourth Sunday of Lent: Gospel, Jn 3:14–21 (God sent his Son to save the world)

Fifth Sunday of Lent: first reading, Jer 31:31–34 (God will conclude a new covenant)

YEAR C

First Sunday of Lent: Gospel, Lk 4:1–13 (The temptation of Jesus)

Second Sunday of Lent: Gospel, Lk 9:28b–36 (The transfiguration of Jesus)

Fifth Sunday of Lent: first reading, Is 43:16–21 (The crossing of the Red Sea)

This division of material makes it possible to develop the principal themes of the Easter Vigil. At the same time, the distribution over the three years of the cycle prevents any given Sunday of Lent from being overloaded.

In the homily of the Easter Vigil the themes treated during Lent are further developed and completed.

Ingobert Jungnitz

Homily Series for Year A

INTRODUCTION TO THE THEMES OF THE HOMILY
SERIES FOR THE THIRD, FOURTH, AND FIFTH
SUNDAYS OF LENT

On the Way to the Feast of Our Liberation
The Easter penitential season (Lent) is, as its very name
indicates, a preparation for Easter. Easter is *the* feast of
Christianity. In observing it we not only recall the suffering and death of Jesus; we also celebrate his resurrection. We believe that the effect of those historical events
reaches to all times and places and that we today are
touched by their power. Their effect is that every person who belongs to Christ is a redeemed person, or to
put it another way, a liberated person. But liberated
from what? This is the burning question asked by
human beings who experience themselves as subject to
unavoidable and apparently insuperable forces. If the
answer given be simply: "from sin and everlasting
death," it sounds like a mere promise of consolation in
the hereafter.

But in fact the practice of the Easter penitential season
militates against the view that the work of Christ was
directed to liberation *solely* at the last judgment. (We
should however also bear in mind that the early Christians looked for Christ to come again during the Easter
Vigil.)

During Lent we prepare to celebrate Easter worthily as
the feast of the great liberation that has already begun.
Through practices of self-denial, we endeavor to escape

the grip of less desirable or even evil habits. Through critical reflection on the discrepancy between the demands of a Christian life and our own patterns of behavior, we prepare for sacramental or extrasacramental reconciliation with the God in whose sight we have become guilty. Through deeds of love for neighbor (*Misereor* fast and collection; family day of fasting), we acknowledge that we take seriously Christ's words about our obligations to our fellow human beings, and thus we strengthen our union with Christ himself, who wishes to redeem or liberate both us and our neighbors.

During the Easter Vigil we will then call to mind the entire history of the human race. It is the history of a divine plan of salvation that cannot be frustrated by human efforts to the contrary; the history of God's irresistible saving action on behalf of this world. We will see clearly that Christ is indeed the light of our world and that the bath of baptism cleanses us for a vital communion with the Holy One whose members we are to some extent privileged to become.

Each of the gospels of the coming Sundays can be heard and understood in isolation and can give us instruction on a life lived according to the will of Jesus. But we wish here to inquire of these gospels what they have to say to us about our Easter celebration. If we are sufficiently attentive to them, we will realize that all three deal in various ways with the fundamental theme of our faith: the fact that Jesus Christ came to liberate the *whole* person from *every* evil.

THIRD SUNDAY OF LENT

Gospel, John 4:5–42—The Water of Christ

Eternal Life through the "Water of Christ"

It is clear, even at a first hearing, that this gospel is a lengthy discussion about water. In the Near East water means life: if there is enough water, there is also enough food to eat; if water is lacking or ceases to fall as rain, then life is threatened or even rendered impossible. It is therefore a piece of truly Good News that the Messiah, the Savior and Redeemer sent by God, has the power to give an inexhaustible supply of living and life-giving water. Moreover, Jesus makes an astonishing claim: that what the tradition of the fathers tells us (remember that this conversation takes place at the ancient and venerable well of Jacob) is not enough, nor does it represent the best that is possible. No, the Messiah—and Jesus professes himself to be the Messiah—is able to offer a source of life that transcends anything thus far known: a gift that can bring everlasting life and forever satisfy all earthly needs.

During the Easter Vigil we will learn what water it is that brings eternal life: the water of baptism. During the Vigil we will be sprinkled with newly blessed water as a reminder of our baptism. But we must also open our minds and hearts to the admonition that this life is not to be obtained in an automatic way. We will profess that the baptism we once received has value only if through faith we accept and commit ourselves to Jesus and his message, and only if we constantly renounce, in a complete and radical manner, the enemy of the divine life that is in us. Christ will give us the water, that is, the life; it depends on us whether this spring of water will turn into a river that carries us ever deeper into the life of God.

This Christ-given Life Emancipates Us from Social Barriers

The liberation from death which Jesus bestows through baptism is not meant to benefit the individual alone. In the gospel pericope he is speaking to a woman who stands outside the religious and national order of Israel to which he himself belongs. Thus it is made clear that the water Jesus offers is not intended only for a limited group. The liberation from the limit which death sets for our normal lifespan is at the same time a liberation from social barriers.

There is no doubt, of course, that our Easter Vigil celebration links us in many ways with the ancient Jewish celebration of liberation, during which the Jews commemorated the Exodus from Egypt and the entrance into the Promised Land, the country God had vowed to give them. At the same time, however, it is clear that our celebration, which has Christ as its focus, is the celebration of a new people of God which is gathered from every people, tribe, and nation. We should therefore ask ourselves what we must still do in order that, in our part of the world and in a society made up largely of Christians, all national and racial barriers may be eliminated. We should remember too that even within our Christian world we have to overcome many religious and confessional barriers through ecumenical thought and action, thus following the example of Christ, who regarded himself as united with the Samaritan woman by a common faith in Yahweh, even though he was separated from her by the different form which the testimony of faith took in each case.

The Need of Greater Concern for God's Work

There is a further statement in this gospel that we should take to heart. Jesus is sent (he tells us) to accomplish God's work. He has indeed brought this work to completion in the events of his death and resurrection, to the extent that in principle no one is now excluded from the water of baptism which bestows a share in the life of God. But salvation does not come automatically. Even those who have been baptized must continue to cultivate the hope that they will one day share fully in Christ's victory over death and in his life in God. One expression of this hope would be for a larger number of Christians to participate in the Easter Vigil celebration this year than last.

Gospel, John 9:1–41—Enlightened by Christ

Blind "for the Sake of Others"—Enlightened by Christ

We often find it difficult to grasp the fact that our life and destiny are part of a larger whole. It is understandable, then, that we should look for a completely individualistic explanation of why a particular person is handicapped. In this gospel, however, Jesus sharply rejects an individualistic explanation of why a particular man has been born blind. He tells us that no concrete individual's sin can account for the man's condition; his blindness is not a punishment for sins committed by the man himself nor for the sins of his parents. And yet in cases of misfortunes involving no guilt (for example, when parents have a handicapped child), we still hear people say of the parents: "They've been punished enough."

Jesus makes it clear that this man is blind "for the sake of others." This is, his lot in life and especially his meeting with Jesus are to become for those around him the means of a new and unparalleled revelation of God.

The saving action which Christ performs—and on a Sabbath at that—points to the fact that he is the "Light of the world." The blind man receives his sight "for the sake of others," that is, in order that others may be enlightened and that a "light may shine" on those around: Christ the Light of the world.

The Easter liturgy will bring home to us even more fully that Christ is the Light of the world. The Easter candle is one of the most eloquent of all the symbols of Christ. Those who believe in him receive a share of his light. They are to bring this light back home with them from the Vigil celebration and carry it through the night, the night of those people to whom the fire of the Easter mysteries means little or nothing. It is clear from this that we too are enlightened "for the sake of others."

"A Christian is a man for others." A short statement, yet it is a program for our entire lives. It is not, however, a program we choose for ourselves, but a program chosen for us by God. Only through Christians will the salvific will and saving action of God be proclaimed. But it is precisely in thus being there "for others" that our own lives acquire their full meaning.

Cooperation in the Work of Redemption

Once again we are told, in passing as it were, that without our active readiness to cooperate in God's work of salvation we get nowhere. The blind man must go to the pool and wash himself. Christ's offer of salvation would have been useless to him if he had not believed, trusted, and done what Christ told him to do.

The saving sacrament of baptism, the sacrament in which the Christ, the Light of the world, enlightens us, is valueless to responsible human beings if they do not accept the consequence of this enlightenment, namely, a renunciation of the powers of darkness such as is required in the renewal of baptismal promises by those celebrating the Easter Vigil.

At the same time, however, this renunciation makes it clear that we would be helpless against the powers of darkness if we were left to our own resources. For as we make this renunciation we hold lighted candles that have been lit from the Easter candle, the symbol of Christ.

FIFTH SUNDAY OF LENT

Gospel, John 11:1–45—Liberation from the Power of Death

He Who Has Been Liberated Can Liberate Others

"Your son . . . loved the world and died for our salvation" (Opening Prayer of the day). This was a great scandal to the disciples of Jesus: the inexorable necessity of this death. Only in the light of Easter and their experience of the resurrection of Jesus did the disciples realize what his death and resurrection had accomplished: "This is the night when Jesus Christ broke the chains of death and rose triumphant from the grave" (Exsultet).

I said last Sunday that "a Christian is a man for others." This holds in a special way for Christ himself, who out of love for the world (that is, first and foremost for human beings), handed himself over to death. When he broke the chains of death he did so for the entire world and became the firstborn from among the dead. For this reason, the feast of his resurrection is the feast of our own resurrection as well. For this reason, too, the joy that marks the liturgy of the Easter Vigil is an anticipation of the joy that will accompany the final victory of each of us over seemingly inescapable death.

In order that the disciples might be able to believe that he is truly risen from the dead and that they might believe that his victory over death means their own victory as well, he gave them a sign: the raising of Lazarus. The details reported in the gospel, the description of Lazarus' subjection to the processes associated with death (corruption, wrapping in gravecloths), the calling of this man forth from the depths of the tomb—all this was a sign that Jesus indeed has the power to liberate human beings from the bonds of death.

We Must Cooperate in Our Liberation

Once again we are told that our liberation by Jesus from the bonds of death requires our cooperation. The gospel of John tells us in moving words that Lazarus had been a friend of Jesus. The depth of human feeling involved in this relationship becomes clear when we see Jesus angered by his death and then weeping for him. The choice of Lazarus to serve as sign of Jesus' power over death was probably due to the fact that he had been Jesus' friend.

This account should, I think, make it clear that our own friendship with Jesus is an indispensable condition of our becoming victors over death. "In his love for us all, Christ gives us the [Easter] sacraments to lift us up to everlasting life," says the Preface for the Fifth Sunday. I have already spoken of the need of our making our baptism effective by renewing our baptismal promises. This conscious commitment to an effective baptism and, as a consequence, our fruitful participation in the Eucharist, are sealed, or perhaps even made possible, by reception of the sacrament of Penance.

The final victory over the power of death, to which all of us must, like Christ, bow for a time, can thus be achieved only through cooperation with Jesus and in a union of friendship with him. Renewal of the power of baptism in us and table fellowship with the risen Lord are possible only through (sacramental or extrasacramental) penance.

If we cooperate in this way in the work of our redemption, the words of the Easter Proclamation will truly apply to us: "This is the night when Christians everywhere, washed clean of sin and freed from all defilement, are restored to grace and grow together in holiness" (Exsultet).

SUGGESTIONS FOR AN EASTER VIGIL HOMILY

1. If the theme of liberation has been developed on the Sundays of Lent, then the best point of departure for an Easter Vigil homily is the eighth reading, the passage from the Letter to the Romans (6:1–11). The theme of the homily might then be: "He who has died is now free."

2. The symbolism of baptism as a death can be emphasized in this passage from Romans. Our death to sin is in fact an act of liberation which God performs. Through this death human beings are set free for a life that is lived for God.

3. God's act of liberation must be completed by the baptized themselves. "Death to sin" is, after all, not a purely spiritual event, inasmuch as sin affects the human person in its entirety. Liberation from the soul's guilty state must therefore be shown to be real and effective by the fact that those now liberated cooperate as best they can in eliminating the corporal effects of sin: in eliminating, for example, all the afflictions of which human beings are in whole or in part the causes.

Homily Series for Year B

SECOND SUNDAY OF LENT

First Reading, Genesis 22:1–2, 9a, 10–13, 15–18—The Firstborn Offered in Sacrifice

The story of the sacrifice of Isaac is a masterpiece of Old Testament narrative art. In today's reading the story is unfortunately condensed, but in five weeks' time, during the liturgy of the word for the Easter Vigil, we will hear it in full. But, unfortunately again, it is almost never read at all during the Easter Vigil; because of the seven Old Testament readings, half are usually omitted in order to keep the service from being too long.

In any case, the story is sufficiently well-known. Many people find it a disturbing story: how could God require a man to sacrifice his own son? But in this objection the significance of the story in the history of salvation is, for practical purposes, completely ignored. In addition, we Christians are usually anti-Semites, even if we do not acknowledge this fact even to ourselves. For this reason we are hardly capable of understanding that to the Jewish mind the story of Isaac relates a key event in the history of salvation. Its importance can be seen from the fact that the sacrifice of Isaac, like the covenant "between the pieces" (Gen 15:9ff.), is transposed to the night of Passover. The sacrifice of Isaac might even be called the "original Easter" that occurred even before the Pasch (= passage) at the Exodus (Ex 12:11). The early Church was aware of the importance of Isaac; its Bible, after all, was for centuries coextensive with the Old Testament. Early Christians, therefore, saw what had happened to Isaac as being fulfilled in Jesus, the crucified and risen firstborn son.

The Firstborn Son

How long Abraham had waited for a son! Through this son the promise made to him would be fulfilled, and he would become the father of a great people as numerous as the grains of sand on the seashore and the stars in the heavens. And now God was asking that this firstborn son be given back to him!

God's claim on the firstborn was beyond dispute: "Whatever is the first to open the womb among the people of Israel, both of man and of beast, is mine" (Ex 13:2). The firstborn must be sacrificed: "Every firstborn of man among your sons you shall redeem" (Ex 13:13). Why was this? Because Abraham had acted thus.

Therefore, the Israelites offered a *lamb* as a substitute, just as Abraham had substituted a ram for his son. This lamb appears again on the night of Passover, when its blood, smeared on the doorposts of Israelite homes, ransoms their firstborn sons. But only the descendants of Abraham are saved; the Egyptians lose their firstborn. But all this was only a prefiguration, because:

The only and beloved son of God is Jesus. The voice from the cloud at the transfiguration tells us this (today's gospel: Mk 9:7). God hands him over as a sacrifice of expiation for the sins of the world. The Son accepts crucifixion and dies in obedience to his heavenly Father. By his death the entire human race is saved.

The Son Sacrificed

The story of the sacrifice of Isaac is doubtless a sacred narrative that explains the existence of a place of worship. Down to our own day, places of pilgrimage appeal for their legitimation to visions once granted there. According to Jewish tradition Moriah is identical with the mountain on which the temple of Jerusalem was built. Here Araunah the Jebusite had a threshing-floor, and David bought it from him in order to build a house of the Lord there. The spot is still the central point of the cathedral-like rock formation over which a resplendent golden cupola now rises. In all probability, it was on this rock that the altar of sacrifice stood in Solomon's temple.

Isaac was *the first sacrifice* to be offered on this spot, to which God had directed Abraham. "Then Abraham put forth his hand, and took the knife to slay his son" (v. 10). Contrary to the biblical text, Jewish tradition even assumed that Isaac had actually been slain in sacrifice. For this reason he was regarded as the "servant of God" and the model of all Jewish martyrs.

The *election and redemption of Israel* had its origin in the blood of Isaac. Every sacrifice that would later be offered through the centuries in the temple was effective for salvation because of its relation to Isaac, the first to be sacrificed on this spot. Even the Passover lamb, slain each year in commemoration of the Exodus, called to mind the blood of Isaac.

The *blood of Jesus*, shed on the cross for us, redeemed all human beings, for God "did not spare his own Son but gave him up for us all" (second reading: Rom 8:32). His sacrifice surpassed all other sacrifices and made them superfluous. From the rising of the sun to its setting this sacrifice will be offered until the end of time as an abundantly efficacious oblation.

The Son Raised Up

The noncanonical Book of Jubilees (second century B.C.) was well-known in the early Church. It is expressly said there, in explanation of the joy of Passover, that Abraham received his son back "on the third day." Perhaps the Letter to the Hebrews is alluding to this conception of what happened to Isaac when it says: "By faith Abraham . . . offered up Isaac . . . . He considered that God was able to raise men even from the dead; hence he did receive him back and this was a symbol" (10:17–19).

Salvation from death is the reward of Abraham's faith. Abraham had said to his servants: "I and the lad will go yonder and worship, and come again to you" (v. 5). He went in order to slay his son, but he expected nonetheless to find life there. No wonder, then, that Abraham became father of the faith of Jews, Muslims, and Christians.

Preservation from death was granted the people of Israel through the blood of the Passover lamb. Enslavement in Egypt had been an experience worse than death for them. The Exodus, therefore, meant not only a rescue from destruction but a resurrection and a new life.

Christ, *the true Passover Lamb*, was offered in sacrifice, but God raised him up again to immortal life. Being himself saved from death he saves us too from it. For by his blood we have been "ransomed for God from every tribe and tongue and people and nation" (Rev 5:9).

In this way did God "perform the mercy promised to our fathers, and . . . remember his holy covenant, the oath which he swore to our father Abraham" (Lk 1:72–73). What Isaac was for the Jews, Jesus Christ is for us: he was raised on the third day and is the cause of our joy and our resurrection.

FOURTH SUNDAY OF LENT

Gospel, John 3:14–21—The Easter Faith
In the gospels of the past three Sundays something was always happening. We listened first to the richly detailed story of the temptation of Jesus. Then Mark led us to the mountain of the transfiguration. A week ago it was the dramatic scene in which Jesus whipped the tradesmen and moneychangers from the temple. This

selection of incidents was not motivated by any desire for sensationalism nor, on the other hand, was it merely accidental. Those readings, like today's, were intended to bring us closer to the Easter mystery.

The passage for today seems indeed, at first hearing, to be much more difficult. It is really a meditation of John on the conversation of Jesus with Nicodemus. John reflects on the One who comes from heaven to bring life. The most important factor, in his judgment, is faith, a term that occurs no less than five times in these few verses.

The Way to Faith

The selection of readings becomes understandable only when we realize that the whole of Lent originally served as a preparation for baptism. During these weeks, the instruction of the catechumens became more intensive, as the candidates received what might be called their final polishing. This instruction was concerned primarily with a review of themes that were of essential importance to faith.

The *crucified* Jesus was therefore the focus of the instruction, since he is the center of our Christian faith. Paul can sum up the whole message in a few words: "We preach Christ crucified" (1 Cor 1:23). Today's gospel from John recalls how at one point in the journey through the wilderness Moses set up a pole with a bronze serpent on it, so that anyone who should gaze on it might be healed. Similarly, the cross is not only a tree of death but a sign of salvation, and everyone who believes receives life from it.

When Jesus was *lifted up*, it was not simply on a tree of shame that he hung, near the city-gate on a rocky hill where all could see him. For his death was at the same time a being lifted up to the Father and a participation in the Father's glory. No wonder, then, that for centuries, believing firmly as they did in an exalted Lord,

Christians did not venerate a cross that depicted the dying or dead Jesus of Nazareth. And when they did at last begin to venerate the cross, they depicted Jesus in the attitude of a conqueror, seeing him as the victor who has overcome death and now gives believers eternal life.

For adult candidates, Easter, the feast of their baptism, was a profound experience. Through baptism they were drawn into the mystery of the death and resurrection of Jesus. The old self died in them when they were immersed in the water, and their emergence from the font was a symbol of their rebirth to a new and unending life. As a sign of this new life they wore their white garments until the following Saturday. Often enough, their reception into the Church meant exclusion from their own families or the surrender of a previous profession or trade. They knew from experience that faith does not come cheaply.

The Necessity of Faith

In all likelihood none of us here was baptized during the Easter Vigil. Certainly the majority of us were brought to the church as tiny infants. No one asked us whether we wanted to be baptized; instead our godparents answered for us as our representatives. Neither were we asked about our faith. But is it that simple a matter to become a Christian? How in fact were we educated to faith and Christian life?

Real belief *in Christ* is not the same as the kind of thing we hear in certain popular sayings: "Of course, I believe in God!" "After all, we all have the same God!" "If only they had some kind of belief!" Is it really possible for all to reach beatitude in their own way? The gospel, for its part, is quite unambiguous on this point: "He who believes in me is not condemned; he who does not believe is condemned already because he has not believed in the name of the only Son of God" (v. 18).

For Christians, to believe *in God* means to believe in the Father of our Lord Jesus Christ. For this God sent his Son into the world to save it; he allowed this Son to die on the cross for us, but he also raised him up as the firstborn from among the dead. The Son thereby became our life, and we received the beginnings of this life in baptism.

As the feast of the resurrection, *Easter* is thus always an occasion for us to renew our baptism. The mere fact of having been baptized is not enough. The adolescent and the adult must repeatedly try to make their baptism truly their own. But in the celebration of Easter day as the older folk among us remember it, and even in what used to be called the "Resurrection Service," the renewal of baptism was hurried through much too quickly. When, therefore, during the Easter Vigil we experience and celebrate the victory of light over darkness, the triumph of life over death, we have every reason to rejoice, because Christ himself is our new life.

The Life of Faith

No one will deny that we do not become authentic Christians simply by writing "Catholic" or "Protestant" on a personal data sheet. Even if we can say that, yes, we were baptized and that, yes, many years ago perhaps, we received first communion and were confirmed, were married in the church and intend to have a Christian burial, all this is not enough to make us genuine Christians. To be a Christian means several things.

It means, first, *to live like Christ*. As a matter of fact, that is precisely what the very name "Christian" means, or at least it implies some similarity to Christ. The name "Christian" was first given to the disciples of Jesus at Antioch because they resembled Christ. But in what does this likeness consist? It required, above all, the kind of obedience to God's will that Jesus practiced throughout his life. It requires the kind of love for human beings that he showed to the poor and the sick, the outcast and the sinner. It requires a readiness for the cross and death, and a life lived in the hope of glory.

Being a Christian means, secondly, *doing the truth*, as the gospel puts it. But what does this somewhat strange phrase signify? It means that there must be no contradiction between what we say and what we do. Our profession of faith must not be mere lip-service. Anyone who claims to believe but in fact does evil will not come to the light. Our deeds must be done in God; only then shall we come to the light.

Easter is the feast of light. When we light our individual candles from the Easter candle, we are indicating that we love light more than darkness; that we are enlightened by Christ who came into the world to be its light. Such should be our experience whenever we proclaim his death and celebrate his resurrection as the mystery of our faith. In every celebration of the Eucharist he gives himself to us as the pledge of true life. We must show our faith in God by living in the light.

In no other liturgy do we experience this so fully and deeply as in the liturgy of the Easter Vigil. We still have three weeks ahead of us before the Vigil. Can anyone here say that he or she has no more to do by way of preparation for that celebration of our faith?

FIFTH SUNDAY OF LENT

First Reading, Jeremiah 31:31–34—*The New Covenant*
The promise of a new covenant is a climactic moment in the Book of Jeremiah and indeed in all of Old Testament prophecy. This text, however, in addition to being rather little known to most of us, was written over 2,500 years ago and in a situation completely outside of our experience.

Jeremiah wrote toward the end of the seventh century B.C. King Josiah, a devout man, had begun a religious revival. The book of the Law of Moses, or the Torah, had been rediscovered in the temple, and the people had committed themselves once more to the covenant made at Sinai. But the initial enthusiasm soon began to flag. The infidelity of the people in their relationship with Yahweh made some coming catastrophe almost certain, and in fact such a catastrophe came upon Judah in 587 B.C. when Jerusalem was captured, the temple destroyed, and the people led away into captivity at Babylon. It was in this situation of decline and exile that the prophet raised his voice and proclaimed God's new offer of salvation.

The Promise of Yahweh

In the Fourth Eucharistic Prayer the celebrant says: "Again and again you offered a covenant to man." While there is an allusion here to Noah and Abraham, the primary reference is to the covenant at Sinai, of which the Book of Exodus contains several reports, each viewing it from a different angle. We read of a banquet being celebrated on the mountain, of the people accepting the covenant, and of Yahweh making the covenant with Moses as the representative of the people. Through this covenant, Israel entered into an entirely special relationship with Yahweh, its God. But how did the covenant turn out?

Complaints about *violations of the covenant* became frequent and bitter: "My covenant . . . they broke, though I was their husband" (v. 32). The sin of Israel was its failure to obey the Law and its rebellion against Yahweh. Above all, Israel violated the basic obligation of the covenant: "You shall have no other gods before me." As a result, the covenant that had been intended for the salvation of the people became their downfall.

The *law of vengeance* now replaced the covenant of forgiveness. Because the people sinned Yahweh had to show himself their master and punish them. The pressure of enemies from the north and the east, the growing superiority of these foes, the threatening catastrophe that soon became unavoidable and ended with the exile and a new enslavement: all these were signs that the covenant had been broken.

The new covenant is a new *gift from Yahweh*. But this new covenant will be different than the one Yahweh had entered into with their fathers. Even the covenant of King Josiah had still been a bilateral contract: "You have declared this day concerning the Lord that he is your God . . . and the Lord has declared this day concerning you that you are a people for his own possession. . . " (Deut 26:17–19). The new covenant will be the doing of Yahweh alone. But it will be a long time before the promise is fulfilled.

The Fulfillment in Jesus Christ

The new and superior covenant stands in contrast to the covenant made at Sinai. In the Letter to the Hebrews, Ps 110 is interpreted as referring to Christ and his being appointed an eternal priest by God. It is said of him in this passage of the letter that he is "the surety [or guarantee] of a better covenant" (Heb 7:22). Consequently he also becomes "the source of eternal salvation" (Heb 5:9), as today's second reading tells us.

The *establishment* of the new covenant does not, of course, simply abrogate the old covenant. For "the gifts and the call of God are irrevocable" (Rom 11:29). The promise had been directed to the people of Israel, and this people has not been cast off. There is no difference in content between the old and new covenants. The covenant formula is identical: "I will be their God, and they shall be my people" (Jer. 31:33).

The *forgiveness of sins* becomes the basis of the new covenant: "I will forgive their iniquity, and I will remember their sin no more" (v. 34). It does not follow from this that there will be freedom from all sin. The point is rather that the power of sin, which compels human beings to resist God, is broken in principle.

The *blood of the covenant* is no longer the blood of oxen and sheep and goats, as in the covenants of Abraham and Moses. The mediator and the ritual for concluding the covenant are not even mentioned in Jeremiah. We do know, however, from the fulfillment of the promise, that Jesus has "made peace by the blood of his cross" (Col 1:20). The Lord, once lifted up, has drawn all to himself (today's gospel: Jn 12:13).

The New Israel

The idea of covenant represents Israel's experience of its God. The experience of the incarnation of the Word and of redemption through Jesus Christ leads the author of the First Letter of Peter to conclude that we are now a people and God's own possession: formerly not a people, but now God's people (1 Pet 2:9–10). "We are the temple of the living God . . . 'I will be their God, and they shall be my people'" (2 Cor 6:16).

In Hearts, Not on Altars: In the Ark of the Covenant in Solomon's temple there were stored the stone tablets with the law of the covenant written on them. In the new covenant, however, God teaches his people interiorly so that each individual will understand and accept his instruction. Now too conversion is a necessary prerequisite for the gifts of salvation. But God speaks to the heart of each person through his Spirit.

Baptism Instead of Circumcision: A visible, bodily sign distinguished the members of the covenanted people from the pagans around them. Now, however, acceptance into the covenant comes through conformity with the mediator of this new covenant. The celebration of his death and resurrection becomes the feast of the covenant at which the faithful are reborn from water and the Holy Spirit, so that "all who are buried with

Christ in the death of baptism [may] rise also with him to newness of life" (blessing of water for baptism).

Eucharist Instead of Holocaust: Ever since the time of Abraham and Moses the people of God had expressed their giving of themselves to God, and therefore their fidelity to the covenant, through sacrifices. The new covenant has been sealed by the sacrificial death of Jesus on the cross. Jesus anticipated his sacrifice in the institution of the Eucharist, where he gave his disciples the cup to drink. From this cup they drank "the blood of the new and everlasting covenant for the forgiveness of sins." Whenever the Eucharist is celebrated, the new covenant is renewed; the new Israel is manifested and becomes the Church.

The promise of salvation recorded in Jeremiah has thus been fulfilled in a superabundant way. In fact, Ezekiel had already carried the promise in Jeremiah a step further when he communicated a new word from God: "I will take out of your flesh the heart of stone and give you a heart of flesh" (Ezek 36:26). The exalted Lord gave his Spirit to his Church, and thus the love of God was poured into our hearts (Rom 5:6).

Johann Peschek

Homily Series for Year C

FIRST SUNDAY OF LENT

Gospel, Luke 4:1–13—*Temptation*

Goal: Today, on the first Sunday of Lent, we are to have before our eyes one of the principal goals of the paschal renewal. We are to begin preparing today for the baptismal promises of the Easter Vigil which represent our constant effort to give ourselves wholly to God. I shall therefore be linking the gospel for the first Sunday of Lent with some thoughts from the fourth, fifth, and sixth readings of the Easter Vigil.

A Vital Context

In our preaching we should always look for a concrete point of contact, something that is of vital interest to the people in their present situation. Then we will be able to make our theme meaningful to them.

An example: for Polish Christians Nowa Huta was both a temptation and a challenge. Close by Cracow one of the great Polish workingmen's cities was to be built from the ground up: without a church, without a cross, without God. The temptation for Polish Christians was to do nothing, because there was no hope of building a church in this new city against the will of the authorities. And yet one day a huge cross stood in the open space, and people gathered around this cross Sunday after Sunday. Nothing could keep them from it. Not rain or snow, not heat or cold. And today there stands on this spot the famous church of Nowa Huta in which every Sunday, from 6 A.M. to 12 noon, there may be as many as 25,000 people celebrating the Eucharist. Someone resisted temptation and believed against all obstacles.

What Is Temptation?

In simple terms, a temptation is an inducement to sin. As such, it can take a thousand forms. An apparently fuller life may be a temptation; an escape from an impasse, the discarding of a burden, the possibility of a new wish-fulfillment (an abortion, a divorce and remarriage)—all these may be forms temptation takes. But temptation can take still other forms: a doubt as to whether God has really forbidden something that promises happiness (the temptation in the Garden of Eden); an unsettling challenge as to whether something is really to be believed or whether something else is really a sin. Then again, temptation may come in the form of a lethargy and discouragement about whether a cause in which I truly believe will ever really succeed, since the trend of things is against it.

Temptation is an impulse to seek personal fulfillment without reference to God. Temptation is the pressure to stop looking any more for a clear vision of God amid the ground mists of earthly life and to be instead a practical person who chooses the lesser of two evils.

The Temptation of Jesus

The ultimate meaning of every temptation becomes clear in the temptation of Christ. Jesus is tempted precisely as Messiah, and this in a very personal and existential way. (We should note, by the way, that the gospel says: Satan "departed from him until an opportune time" [v. 13]. This implies that Jesus had been tempted before and would be tempted again. After all; he became like us in everything except sin.)

Jesus knows the road he must travel. He knows all that

73

lies ahead of him in order that the scriptures may be fulfilled. The devil, whose natural intelligence has not been affected by his fall, tries personally to cloud the picture. "Command this stone to become bread" (v. 3), he says to a man who has been fasting for forty days. "Throw yourself down from here [the pinnacle of the temple]; for it is written, 'He will give his angels charge of you. . .' and 'On their hands they will bear you up'" (vv. 9–11). Then the people who see this marvelous thing will make you king: such is the suggestion the devil makes to the Messiah, who can in fact save only those who trust and believe in him. Finally, since Jesus is ready to empty himself completely, the tempter decides to test his humility, and say to him: "Worship me" and for this simple, painless action I will give you the entire world and you in turn can give it back to the Father. Here the devil plays the clever manager; under his guidance the whole business will be done more smoothly, more effortlessly and more expeditiously. But in God's plan redemption must be by the arduous way of the cross and through tangled conflicts; it requires waiting for his hour to come.

The Meaning of All Temptation

In the temptation of Jesus the ultimate meaning of all temptation comes to light. Just as Satan's radical decision to achieve his fulfillment without God turned his existence precisely into something "satanic," so in every temptation the issue is whether human beings will seek their apparent fulfillment apart from God and in opposition to his plans. In Paradise, the first couple on their own authority ate from the tree of knowledge, without waiting for God's permission. Now Christ, the Messiah, is tempted to choose his own way of carrying out his task. But Jesus refuses even to discuss the matter. He immediately takes the Father's side once and for all: "Man shall not live by bread alone"; "You shall not tempt the Lord your God."

For Jesus, then, temptation is a challenge to give himself completely to the Father and to the Father's will.
He prefers to drink the chalice rather than travel the
more comfortable and simpler road that in the final
analysis is not a road at all. The world must be made to
realize the value to be set on the Father's love. Thus
temptation has two meanings. From Satan's standpoint
it is an incitement to godlessness. From God's
standpoint it is a challenge to decide wholly for him. In
this sense God himself can "tempt" us. In fact he must
go on tempting us so that we may come to the point of
an unreserved decision to love him with all our heart,
with our senses and mind, and with all our strength. To
the God who gives everything, we human beings can
reply only by giving him all in return.

The Characteristic Temptation of Our Time

Do we not see in the experience of Christ an indication
of the characteristic threats to our existence as Christians in the affluent society? Temptation blurs the difference between a raising of the living standard that is
truly willed by God and a satanically inspired softness
that quenches the spirit and weakens the backbone.
People today are told they must use technology to overcome the practical problems of life and need no longer
look to the spiritual realm for the acquisition of moral
values. The Church is tempted to evade the unpleasant
and uncomfortable job of telling people that the easier
way is often sinful and that God is reached only by a
hard road. The Church is tempted to remain silent
when there seems little likelihood that people will listen
to a more demanding message.

A Look Ahead to the Easter Vigil

The fourth, fifth, and sixth readings of the Easter Vigil
describe the situation of those who have made the
wrong decision in time of temptation and have not met
the challenge given them by God. The fourth reading

describes Israel as a people to which God was close as he was to no other, but which abandoned God and has now itself become like "a wife forsaken and grieved in spirit." Israel is now "storm-tossed." If the Israelites admit their wrong decision and turn back to God, he will accept them back with great compassion. The fifth reading of the Vigil tells us that human beings pay money for what does not nourish or fill them. In temptation they choose the seemingly better part from which God is missing. If they leave the path of error and thirst again for the true way, they will be able to reach the water. The sixth reading is a very striking one. Israel must hear and learn wisdom: "Why is it, O Israel, why is it that you are in the land of your enemies . . . that you are defiled. . . ? You have forsaken the fountain of wisdom." And when Israel does return to God, it is said of her: "Happy are we, O Israel, for we know what is pleasing to God." No other god now has a place alongside the God of Israel, and to no other people is the privileged place of Israel given.

Temptation and the Baptismal Promises in the Easter Vigil

In the light of what I have been saying, the meaning of the baptismal promises renewed at Easter becomes clear. Those who lived Lent with heightened awareness and realize how their lives are subject to temptation; those who acquire insight into their personal temptations and see which are the ones that hit them hardest; those who are painfully aware of their own wrong turnings and want to live a new life: all these have the power to say "No" and mean it without reserve. Protest against sin and against the wrong we do to God by sin is the only form of protest possible for a Christian. Then a strike against Satan and his arts of seduction bears fruit again. The choice of an easier life has proven to be the choice of a less worthwhile life as well, and therefore we now accept the kind of life that is pleasing to God, even if it be also more difficult.

Henceforth we will look upon temptations as "temptations" from God, testings calculated to elicit decisions of love from us. We will ask for the gifts of the Holy Spirit so that amid the mists of life we shall nonetheless keep God clearly before us. Like Jesus, we want to take the Father's side. The more personal, concrete, and committed our decisions are, the more fully we experience who God is, what love, truth, and wisdom really mean, and what peace and joy are. Then we will have the first fruits of the Lord's promise: "Be faithful unto death, and I will give you the crown of life" (Rev 2:10). And our life will be sustained by those grace-inspired decisions that God grants to those who strive for them.

SECOND SUNDAY OF LENT

Gospel, Luke 9:28b–36—Transfiguration

Goal: Our aim today is to prepare for the central mystery that we celebrate in the Easter Vigil: the mystery of the risen and glorified Lord. The basis for our reflections will be the second reading and gospel of this second Sunday of Lent. The same themes recur in the reading from Romans and the gospel of the Easter Vigil.

A Vital Context
When we are able to make use of some happening that takes place at the time we preach a given sermon, some suitable event of the day, we have found the best way of going about our subject. The mystery of the transfiguration of Jesus was the mystery of his interior life that now took hold of his entire humanity, even in its corporeal dimension. We should therefore attempt to gain access to the mystery of the transfiguration by taking the interior life of the human person as our point of departure. One possibility would be to start from the following case of suicide, so typical of our affluent society, in which a pattern becomes visible: the externals of life in abundance, but no interior life capable of giving these externals a meaning.

We recently heard the shocking report that a young man of 21, the only son of a manufacturer, had been found shot by his own hand. This young man had, by external standards, everything that life could offer: plenty of money, a pretty wife, a luxury yacht, and so on. The dead man had left a note in which he told his parents: "You gave me everything —except for one thing: a meaning for my life."

Man Between Two Worlds: The Inner and the Outer

The internal and the external are both essential components of the human person. The human person has and is both dimensions. He is, so to speak, an external world of his own that is shaped, given life, and ensouled from within. Harmony exists within such a being only when the internal and the external are rightly ordered each to the other. They say of Mother Teresa that one day she intended to accompany four of her Sisters to the airport. These four women were going off to be trained in the care of the sick and dying. On the way to the airport they passed a man who lay dying at the roadside. Mother Teresa and the Sisters broke their journey and stayed with the dying man, for Mother Teresa's guiding principle was: "There are people who have not been able to live a life worthy of human beings. We must help them at least to die with human dignity." The Sisters were not unhappy with this turn of events, for they radiated love and peace and were able to communicate it to the dying man.

We catch a glimpse here of a great truth: human beings need an interior life. On the one hand, we see the manufacturer with many external possessions but nothing inside; on the other, the Sisters with few external possessions but a great deal within. Human beings must have an interior life if they are to be happy. That is the point of the message of Jesus who calls the poor blessed and tells us that we should first seek God's reign within us and then everything else will be given in addition.

Affluence and Technology Do Not Create an Interior Life

Everyone enjoys the helps and comforts available in our present-day world. But it is easy to produce external things and difficult to form the inner self; therefore we are readily tempted to create an imposing exterior and neglect the interior. We certainly change the external world today far more than we change our inner selves. An extravagant exterior, but empty desolation within: like Satan's "empty promises" or what used to be called his "pomp." People today have so many ways of distracting themselves and creating diversions; they can consume and lay their plans—and find so little time for prayer, for God, for themselves, and for reflection on their lives. But of what use is it for people to gain the whole world (have every possible external possession) and lose their own souls (when they have no interior life)? The most priceless vase is worthless if it contains nothing for a thirsty man to drink; but fresh clear water tastes delightful even if served in a very ordinary glass.

Interior and Exterior According to Jesus

The message of the Sermon on the Mount is a message about the building up of the inner self. It deals with the pure heart, with interior joy amid external persecution, with compassion, with hunger, thirst, and sorrow. It deals with poverty of spirit. All these are realities of the inner self. Jesus is inexorable, utterly unyielding, when he runs up against the Pharisees who concentrate on externals; he calls them "whitewashed tombs . . . full of dead men's bones" (Mt 23:27). He accuses them: "You cleanse the outside of the cup and of the plate, but inside you are full of extortion and rapacity" (Mt 23:25).

Jesus Concentrates on the Interior

If we examine the career of Jesus, we see that he made no direct change in the external world. He did not attack the foreign occupying power, though this limited the freedom of his people; nor did he overturn the government in Israel, though this was leading the people astray. He did not change society with its practice of slavery and its unequal treatment of women. He did not close down the temple in order to reform its sacrificial liturgy. On the contrary, he cleansed the temple so that it might be once again his Father's house. And yet no other person has ever so greatly altered and transformed history, time, and every area of the world's life.

Jesus began with the inner life of human beings. He began with a woman of whom even an angel was compelled to say: "You are filled with grace!" He began, then, with a human being who once again carried heaven within herself. And at the end of his life he took bread and spoke these simple words over it: "This is my body." From this moment on the externals of bread concealed the greatest possible inward reality: the Lord himself. As our heritage, therefore, he left us this mighty inward reality under the fragile externals of bread. He had his disciples make a novena in Jerusalem before he armed them with the inner life of God himself: with the Holy Spirit.

In his own self and his own earthly life, Jesus was the invisible God himself, a God whom human beings could see, hear, and touch in bodily form. We therefore profess our faith: the Word became flesh. Some of his contemporaries recognized this hidden inwardness and cried out to him: "My Lord and my God!" But others took offense at the externals of a carpenter's son; they mocked the outer man and told him to come down from the cross if he was so powerful. Some took pity on the outer man, as Pilate did, but they nonetheless sacrificed this just man so that their own careers might not be endangered.

The Transfiguration of Jesus: The Interior Is Revealed

Of the twelve apostles, three (we might call them the inner circle) were granted an experience of what Jesus really was interiorly. They were granted this revelation of the Lord's inner self so that his glory might be made manifest to them. Peter had been so deeply moved by this experience that he referred to it many years later in a letter. The apostles had often been profoundly stirred when they experienced the miracles he worked. But here on the holy mountain they saw his interior self take outward form.

Transfiguration and Resurrection

Just as Jesus at the Last Supper anticipated his death on the cross by his giving of himself in the Eucharist, so too he anticipated his resurrection by his transfiguration. He allowed the glory to shine forth that was his by nature and that would make itself definitively known in the resurrection. He was already what he would later be: he was the king of glory, the reflection of the Father, God from God, and Light from Light.

Ways to Inwardness and Transfiguration

Are we convinced that the interior is more important than the exterior? Are we more concerned, for ourselves and for others, about the interior than we are about the exterior? Or is our belly still our God, and do earthly things still fill our minds? Even in its bodily dimension, the final fulfillment of our human existence comes from Jesus Christ, "who will change our lowly body to be like his glorious body" (second reading). Are we convinced that we can and should live, even now, as men and women risen from the dead, as we are told in the reading from Romans in the Easter Vigil: "You also must consider yourselves dead to sin and alive to God in Christ Jesus." As in the caterpillar, pupa and butterfly are already contained in germ and as the tree is already latent in the seed, so too in our innermost selves we are already transfigured and risen in a germinal or seminal way. The more we die to sin now during Lent, the more fully we can live now with Christ in a real way through grace. The transfiguration of the Lord is something that can be experienced in this world. Thus the saints who sincerely sought it experienced God and their own interior life even in the present world. We complain that our experience of faith is minimal, but the reason is that our interior life is impoverished. If we pursued Christ and the kingdom of God with the same energy with which we pursue the things of this world, we would indeed have experiences of God to tell about, and we would be believed because our happiness would show. But in fact we are too unspiritual.

FIFTH SUNDAY OF LENT

First Reading, Isaiah 43:16–21—Crossing

Goal: The third reading of the Easter Vigil is never to be omitted (Ex 14:15 to 15:1). The crossing of the Red Sea is an essential event of salvation in the Old Testament kerygma. We find the same theme taken up in the first reading of the fifth Sunday of Lent. Moreover, the mystery of the crossing and the mystery of Christ's redemptive action are interwoven. Our aim today is to prepare ourselves for the "theology of crossing" proper to the Easter Vigil.

A Vital Context

Our own age has seen and heard the fearful experiences of refugees. People in South Vietnam risk everything in order to escape a horrible fate. They take the dangerous road to the coast, where spies are everywhere. They pay a rescuer who takes them out to sea in his own boat, risking his own life. There they transfer to another boat, spurred on only by the hope that a ship will stop and take them aboard or that they can reach a foreign coast. How happy the few whose flight is successful! They have lost everything, but they have also gained everything. Their crossing has been successful.

Israel's Greatest Hours: Exodus, Crossing, Entry

Today's reading does not allude to the adventurous journey of some individual refugee. It is a whole people that is being led from serfdom, from slavery, to the land promised them. This was a people that had no longer been its own master, that had no freedom, no possibility of shaping its own life on this earth; a people forced to be content with the bare necessities of life. This was a people whose firstborn sons were put to death and whose daughters were sold as slaves. This was a people that possessed nothing but its faith in God and its hope that this God would come to its rescue. The faith was often little indeed and subject to crises and fears, so that only after many purifications was God able to lead the people further.

Once set free, this people acknowledged, at least on its best days, that it owed its existence solely to its God. For this reason it celebrated his feasts year after year. It slew the Passover lamb whose blood had saved it. With traveling belt donned and ready for the journey, it celebrated the Passover meal. It sang in its songs God's victorious rescue at the crossing of the Sea of Reeds. The waters of this sea had been for Israel waters of life and salvation, but for the Egyptians, waters of destruction and death. Israel also celebrated the fulfillment of the promises: the entry into the Promised Land.

In Israel's Crossing Yahweh Revealed Himself

In Israel's commemorations of its rescue and its birth as a nation, God's nearness was manifested over and over again. Israel had to celebrate its past rescue in order to know its God ever anew: to experience him and love him and praise him. In these celebrations God revealed himself to the successive generations of Israelites, for all generations of this people were meant to belong to him. And since these celebrations set a stamp on the entire life of Israel as a society, the Israelite people became a revelation of God to the other peoples.

Israel was duty-bound to proclaim that Yahweh is the living God, the almighty and just God, the God who protects and defends, the God who is merciful and cares for us. God is a saving God, a God infinitely close to us, a God who takes pity on us in our needs. Yahweh does not prevent distress, but he rescues from distress. He is the faithful God who remains faithful even to a people that breaks his covenant, and who in his mercy accepts them when they repent of their straying. For Israel, then, God was a father and a bridegroom. He was the God who marvelously fulfills all his promises.

Israel's Strongest Weapon: The Liturgy

It is an extraordinary fact that this people carries on its struggle by means of its liturgy. Its liturgy is its strongest weapon. This liturgy may be said to be in a sense "sacramental," for it is God who decrees its signs, and the people institute them with believing and loving confidence in him. Then God acts and rescues and fulfills his promises. The signs are powerless in themselves and, to many, even laughable. At the *Exodus* the saving liturgy took the form of the celebration of a Passover meal whose least details were prescribed by God: the lamb was slain and the doorposts smeared with its blood. Israel acts in faith, and then God begins his personal intervention and displays such might that Pharoah, despite all his power, is conquered.

At the *crossing* Moses performs the sign: he lifts his staff, and the people's faith enables them to advance into the sea. Their faith is a faith born of need, for the enemy is at their back; they can only believe and advance. Moses again raises his hand, and the waters become a source of salvation for the Israelites and of destruction for the Egyptians. When the crossing is complete the people become a mighty joyous song of victory.

The *entry* into the Promised Land again takes the form of a single extended liturgy. For six days the people carry the Ark of the Covenant in procession around Jericho. On the seventh day they circle the city seven times, and then the walls of Jericho collapse. Thus the Promised Land is conquered by means of a liturgy which God had decreed; God has given them the city. In light of these events we can understand why the annual liturgy of Passover left such a profound mark on Israelite society and why it means everything to this people. The liturgy was Israel's strongest weapon and a real danger to her enemies. In fact, Israel was so shaped by the liturgy that when the spirit had departed from it she continued to observe it to the letter. At such times as Israel failed to celebrate the liturgy and turned to idolatry, the enemy gained the upper hand. If the liturgy of the covenant was no longer part of Israel's life, then Yahweh would no longer fight for his people.

Israel Lives as Long as It "Journeys"

Behind the talk of Exodus, crossing, and entry there stands a magnificent reality-symbol. In those days Israel had no fixed home, but was a nomadic folk whose leader was God. Life was impossible unless the people moved from one pasture ground to another. And new pasture grounds were to be found only in the midst of their enemies, where God had to prepare the way. Israel could move on only if accompanied by the Ark of the Covenant, that is, by God himself. But the Ark was a continuing challenge to be faithful to the covenant and to live day and night in the presence of the covenant God. Thus the ongoing life of the people was maintained by an onward journey. At the same time, however, the people could journey onward only if they lived the kind of life required of them. Thus everything formed a unity: liturgy, life, journeying.

Liturgy as the Abiding Foundation of Christian Existence, or: We Live to the Extent That We Are Liturgical

What I have been saying should be a stimulus to reflection on our part as the people of the new covenant. The liturgy of the new covenant is even more powerful; it grounds our existence at an even deeper level; and it is more dangerous than the liturgy of Israel. For us the stake is not just earthly life but an eternal and definitive life; the stake is salvation in the fullest sense. We celebrate the fact that the source of our existence is the blood of the Lamb that has rescued and redeemed us.

Every celebration of the Eucharist gives us a share in this saving blood that was poured out for us, a share in the Lamb of God who takes away the sins of the world. In baptism each of us has experienced a "crossing." The waters of baptism have removed sin from us, and these same waters have given us new life, the life that is God's own possession, to the extent that in baptism we have truly become adopted children through grace. We may draw a parallel with the procession around Jericho and say that we grasp the mysteries of our redemption only if we reflect prayerfully on them in our hearts and never grow weary of this effort to understand.

The basis of Christian family life is provided through the liturgy of marriage. The redemptive priesthood and mediatorship of Jesus Christ is made present in time and space through the liturgy of ordination. The liturgy of penance, like a second baptism, repeatedly purifies us and rescues us from the power of darkness into the kingdom of light. In the liturgy of confirmational anointing, the Spirit is given who brings us life in its fullness. The liturgy of the anointing of the sick either rescues us from the overwhelming flood of illness or else transports us across the waters of death to the shore of eternal life.

In the light of all this we can understand what is meant

by saying that a Christian lives to the extent that he or she is liturgical. We can also see how the Christian liturgy parallels the liturgy on which Israelite existence was based. Of course, the liturgy of the new covenant exercises its power only for those Christians who have a life-giving faith. Liturgy without faith is liturgy without a soul; faith without liturgy would mean the absence of the life-giving incarnate Son of God who continues to be active in the sacramental signs. Liturgy that is not the expression of Christian life is a profanation of the holy. That kind of liturgy is dangerous because it brings condemnation.

The Liturgy, Source and Summit of Christian Life

Just think of the effect on the worldwide Church if the whole of Christendom were to celebrate the coming Easter liturgy as it should be celebrated, and were to do so with lively faith and against a background of true Christian life! Just think of the effect on our parish community if each of us were to turn our lives around through genuine repentance and confession and were to celebrate the great saving deeds of God with joyous hearts! Just think of the effect on our individual life if each of us were personally to celebrate Easter with unreserved love! Then God, who has remained with us, would renew his miracles.

THE EASTER VIGIL

Introductory Remark
It is important to note that the themes discussed during Lent—temptation, transfiguration, crossing—are proclaimed again in the readings of the Easter Vigil. The short sermon should come from the heart of the homilist as a personal, existential witness added to the testimonies that are proclaimed in God's scriptural word. The celebration will in this way have the kind of existential character that enables God's word to hit home. The short homily suggested here would perhaps

best be placed just before the renewal of baptismal promises.

Short Homily

It was the supreme happiness of Israelite believers that no god could be as close to his people as Yahweh was to Israel. When the Israelites celebrated Passover, and indeed any of their feasts, they did not simply recall in a dim remote way their people's far-off first love of God and God's far-off first love of Israel. No, their "liturgical remembering" was a calling to mind, a renewal of awareness, that this God was even now very close to them, that he was wholeheartedly present to them as a saving, compassionate, healing, helping, powerful, warrior God. All whose souls were prepared were filled with the realization that Yahweh is the God who *is* (the burning bush), the God who has never set aside his first love, but still bestows it on his people in all its original and everlasting freshness.

Ever since Ash Wednesday, we have been preparing for the climactic moment that is the Easter Vigil. Even more than the Israelites we stand in the presence of God, because his grace has become even greater and his saving deeds even mightier. In the Holy Spirit and with the same irrevocable first love, the Father bestows on each of us his sacrificed and risen Son. Each person who has prepared worthily for this moment is offered the supreme gift of the Father's incomparable love: his transfigured Son. But only those who love in return are capable of receiving this gift that comes from the Father's love. Because the Father has spoken his definitive Yes to us in the person of his Son, only they can worthily go forth to meet him who have over and over again said their Yes to him in the temptations of life and who want during this night to make that Yes a definitive Yes. Let us then resist the evil one with all the strength of our free will and let us commit our lives to God in unconstrained love.

First through the grace of baptism and later through the repeated graces of the sacrament of penance, we have gone forth from the kingdom of darkness. Amid many testings and much distress we have crossed the sea of life and have experienced God's saving love. We now have the privilege of entering into the mighty saving mysteries of God, into the Promised Land which is Jesus Christ himself, the risen and glorified Lord.

We know that every person who now accepts the risen and glorified Lord rises with him, and is glorified and transfigured with him. This is truly what happens to every person who participates in the eucharistic body of the Lord. This new reality fills us even though it does not yet break through the veil as a transformation visible to the senses.

Let us henceforth be no longer two-faced; let us not lead divided lives. Let us not love both God and the "world" or be conformed to both God and the "world." That kind of contradiction, that kind of tension would destroy us. This evening let us once again choose God alone, because he once again chooses us individually in an act of infinite love. In this spirit let us renew our baptismal promises.

III. Celebration

Rudolf Schwarzenberger

Easter: The Feast of Feasts

The Easter Proclamation, or Exsultet, is tireless in its praise of "this holy night." During the Easter Vigil as on no other occasion do the past, present, and future of salvation become present in the liturgical celebration, although this linking of past, present, and future is characteristic of all festivity.

The revised Roman Calendar emphasizes the unity of the Easter triduum (Holy Thursday evening to Easter Sunday evening) and considers the *celebration of the Easter Vigil* to be the center of the three-day celebration. In the Easter Vigil the Church celebrates the *entire paschal mystery*, that is, it celebrates the Lord's passage through suffering and death to resurrection. A repeated effort must therefore be made to turn this celebration into what it really is: *the feast of feasts*.

The question has legitimately been asked: How able are people today to celebrate a feast? Living as they do in a highly technological and rationally organized world, have they not lost the ability to celebrate feasts as they used to do in the past?

I agree with Alexander Schmemann when he says: "Christianity came to birth and was preached in cultures in which feasts and celebrations were an organic and important component of the common worldview and lifestyle." But—our contemporaries ask—are we not now too distant from that time of birth and too far removed from the place where it occurred?

And yet in our time and in this "so very sensible" world of ours, voices are increasingly heard that deny modern man's loss of the ability to celebrate feasts and that insist very emphatically on the importance of festive celebrations for the individual and for the various human communities: family, Church, state, and so on.

The significance of feasts and celebrations for the believers of our day was recently described by theologian W. Kaspar:

"The celebration of the Eucharist gives expression to the truth that in the final analysis we do not derive our life from our own accomplishments but owe it to God. It expresses the truth that human beings do not live solely for work and achievements or for consumption or protests, but find their fulfillment in festivity and celebration. Surely this is a penetrating criticism of our society, and much needed today. There can be no more fully human activity than the celebration of liturgy."

There are probably few who would challenge this assessment. And yet those accepting it will find great difficulty in so celebrating Easter that it truly becomes the feast of feasts. The difficulties do not arise at the level of principle but spring rather from the rhythm of life in our day. Especially in the large cities Easter has become a "long weekend," which urbanites want to spend away from home. This causes a problem in many communities. On the other hand, this same fact provides a pastoral opportunity in places that attract tourists. These are all facts that cannot be ignored, although they should not be an excuse for resignation to the way things are. Even today St. Thomas Aquinas's motto, *Quantum potes, tantum aude* (Be as daring as you can), should guide us in the celebration of the liturgy.

Anyone who wants to *celebrate* the Easter Vigil and not just do his duty by a rubrically correct ceremony must reflect beforehand on several matters.

I am not referring here primarily to the "technical" preparation that is done in the parish's liturgy committee as it plans the celebration of the triduum. I am thinking rather above all of the *kerygmatic preparation* of the entire community by means of preaching and of catechesis of adults, young people, and children. Reference has already been made several times to the importance of the Easter penitential season as a time of "community exercises." Various themes can be taken up during this period, but a biblico-theological and liturgico-theological introduction to these central liturgical celebrations should never be omitted. One reason why the festive character of liturgical celebrations is lost is that the celebration is drowned out in a spate of words which explain what is going on but which also turn the celebration into a course of instruction.

The Easter Vigil celebration certainly requires interpretative explanation, but this should not become the predominant characteristic of it. A good deal can be done by means of a suitable program over a period of time. It is especially inappropriate to explain details of liturgical history during the Vigil celebration, however important and interesting these may be in themselves. The time for that sort of thing is *before* Easter. Liturgy needs an element of re-cognition, and a suitable preparation makes this possible.

During the celebration itself a *mystagogical* type of explanation is best calculated to help the congregation enter into the mystery being celebrated. But even this type of guidance must play a subordinate role and not be a hindrance to the proclamation of the word.

The kind of preparation I have been describing should not be undervalued. Each year it can take a different form: one year, a series of sermons; another year, a course of instruction; in still another, the various media may be used. Where this kind of varied preparation is offered, the community will grow in its understanding of the paschal celebration.

In my opinion, part of a more proximate preparation will be to make the relevant *texts* available and to have the people *learn by memory songs specific* to this liturgical celebration. For on the one hand, it is desirable that the people should hold lighted candles in their hands during a major part of the nocturnal celebration, but on the other, experience shows that it is difficult for them to use hymnals while doing so. A special text for this celebration can be a valuable help to those participating. It is an impossible situation when the people are asked to try new songs just before the celebration.

THE HOUR FOR THE VIGIL CELEBRATION

This really ought to be self-evident. The Sacramentary retains in principle the rule observed in the early Church: "In accord with ancient tradition, *this night is one of vigil for the Lord* (Ex 12:42). The Gospel of Luke (12:35ff.) is a reminder to the faithful to have their lamps burning ready, to be like men awaiting their master's return so that when he arrives he will find them wide awake and will seat them at his table" (Rubrics for the Easter Vigil, no. 1).

"*The entire celebration* of the Easter Vigil *takes place at night*. It should *not begin before nightfall*; it should end before daybreak on Sunday" (no. 3).

As in so many other instances, we have allowed practical considerations to turn a nocturnal celebration into one held on the evening before the feast. But this contradicts the nocturnal character of the Vigil, a character which it has not simply as a matter of liturgical history but for theological reasons.

Anyone who has followed the literature on this subject cannot but admit that all the practical, pastoral considerations cannot outweigh the theological consideration. In this connection it has been correctly observed: "The

96

celebration is a nocturnal celebration, beyond any doubt, but it should carry over to the day, since it is the *Pascha Domini*, the Lord's passage from darkness to light, that is being celebrated" (B. Kleinheyer). From this consideration another writer concludes: "The choice of a time for beginning the celebration of the Easter Vigil is a catechetical statement which cannot be made solely in terms of when the majority of the people may be able to come to the church" (K. Richter). This practical question of the hour for beginning the Vigil celebration shows clearly the importance of a suitable preparation of the community. Unless the biblico-theological and liturgico-theological context is properly understood, it is not possible to answer this question in a proper way.

And yet all who are concerned in this decision are aware of how difficult it is to work out an ideal solution that also does justice to the community.

In any case, there is a minimum requirement: the Easter Vigil celebration is not to be a "Mass on the eve" for Easter Sunday. Therefore the time at which it begins is to be clearly different from other evening services (including Holy Thursday and Good Friday). The prescription in the Sacramentary, that "it should not begin before nightfall" (that is, darkness, not twilight), must not be left unobserved. Much too little attention has hitherto been paid to the possibility of celebrating the Vigil during the final hours of the night, that is, before dawn of Easter Sunday.

THE LENGTH OF THE SERVICE
People who celebrate a feast rarely ask how long it will last. Only in "festive activity" in which they participate from a sense of duty do they sometimes glance unobtrusively at their watches.

This is to say that the primary question concerning the Easter Vigil is not how long it lasts but how it is celebrated. Here again attention must be paid to the meaning of the service: "In accord with ancient tradition, *this night is one of vigil for the Lord* (Ex 12:42)."

This night is thus different "from other nights" not only by the time at which the celebration begins but also by the length of time it takes. Consequently the question of what *must* be unconditionally included by way of song, reading, and actions and what may be omitted is not a good guide for those who want to *celebrate* Easter. Festivity and celebration take time.

And yet if a longer than usual liturgy is not to weary those participating, especially when it is a nocturnal liturgy, the whole liturgical community must become involved in it. The paschal mystery is full of an inner tension and dynamism, and this must find expression in the liturgical celebration.

There has been a great deal of discussion about the structure of the Easter Vigil celebration as found in the new Sacramentary. But in the context of my reflections here I can only refer the reader to this literature.

THE PLACE OF THE CELEBRATION
The church building alone does not meet all the needs of the Easter Vigil.

The Open Space in Front of the Church
For the blessing of the fire and the preparation of the Easter candle, the Easter fire is to be prepared and lit "in a suitable place outside the church."

The place must be a suitable one, that is, it should be a quiet spot and one that has room not only for lighting a pile of wood but for having the congregation gather around it.

This is often difficult in urban churches. A brightly lit, much traveled street in front of the church does not permit a meaningfully symbolic lighting of the new fire. In this case the instruction given in no. 13 of the rubrics is to be followed: the bonfire and the blessing of it are to be omitted and the service of light is to begin at the church door with the lighting of the Easter candle.

In rural communities where the church stands in a churchyard or cemetery no candles should be lit at, for example, the graves of relatives there; such candles may be lit from the Easter candle after the celebration.

The Church
The entire church should be decorated for the feast. Special attention should be given to certain locations because of their role in the Easter Vigil celebration:

1. The spot where the Easter candle is to stand.
2. The place from which the Easter Proclamation is to be sung.
3. The place of baptism; the reference is obviously to a spot that can be seen by the community. Even if there is a special baptistery or a font that cannot be seen by the community, the place chosen for the blessing of the baptismal water and for the baptism itself must be visible to the community, probably in front of the altar or presidential chair.
4. The altar itself.
5. The "holy sepulcher," when local tradition demands that this play a part in the celebration of the Easter Vigil.

THE SYMBOLS OF THE EASTER VIGIL
The question arises not only of modern man's "lack of capacity for celebration" (mentioned earlier) but also of his "lack of capacity for symbols." In a world which is largely artificial and rationally ordered and in which our dealings with nature are almost always at second hand, natural symbols like fire, light, water, and others do not seem to be grasped precisely as symbols. This is, of course, a serious matter for a community that celebrates the liturgy!

The liturgy generally and especially the liturgy of the Easter Vigil "lives" on symbols. But is this not true of our life today, and not just of the liturgy? Many things, and those often the most profound, that move us as human beings—love, tenderness, compassion, agreement, rejection, and so on—find expression in signs more than in words. Not long ago, Joseph Gélineau, one of the "architects" of the liturgical reform, wrote as follows:

"If we want to restore the renovative power of symbols, we must have confidence in the human person as one who lives by symbols. We have no right to assert that the symbols of the liturgy are not accessible to the people of our day. . . . Symbols that are based on the sign character of the body and of nature still have power to move, provided they are *placed in a favorable environment.* . . . A sign acquires its symbolic content only when put in relation to other things. Meaning exists only in totalities. A symbolic action can only be part of a whole within which there are numerous interrelations. . . ."

Our preparation for the Easter Vigil celebration is, in the final analysis, an effort to establish a "favorable environment" wherein signs can become expressive symbols into which the community can enter in an existential way.

The theological "environment" or field has already been described: in the Easter Vigil the Church celebrates the entire paschal mystery, that is, the passage through suffering and death into the glory of the resurrection. The dynamics of the celebration are determined by our new life in Christ. All life is an exodus (a going forth and a crossing) from darkness to light, from death to everlasting life. This is why the liturgy of the Easter Vigil is filled with the symbols of life: light, word, water, meal.

Light

From darkness to light! This is why the time at which the liturgy begins is so important. Mere talk about the darkness of death, with absolutely no accompanying experience of darkness, is worthless. The community ought to be able to "feel" this darkness. Darkness makes it easier to get into a mood (for example, the dimming of the lights in a theater as the play is about to begin). Darkness should therefore reign not only inside the church but outside as well, in the churchyard or the space in front of the church. For this reason, it is better for the congregation to remain in the church if conditions outside are not favorable.

The fire is blessed, the Easter candle is lit, and the flame is passed from the Easter candle: "Christ our light!" All light comes from *him*. We pass it to one another; we become a source of light for one another and then follow *him* together: from the darkness of death into the light of new life.

Word

In our day the psychotherapists have brought home to us how important words are as a symbol of life. Infants and the isolated elderly alike show that without speech, without verbal communication, people cannot live a life worthy of human beings.

A hymn of praise to the lifegiving word of God (the Exsultet) precedes the liturgy of the word in the Easter Vigil. This word rescues, redeems, and gives new life. But God's word calls for a human response, and this response finds expression in the songs between the readings as well as in the congregation's renewed baptismal promises.

Water

Even in the great cities that have now become waterless "steppes," water can be experienced as a symbol of life.

The great cities often suffer periods of drought, and the lack of water can lead to considerable disturbances of civilized order. We even see efforts made to "restore life" to our gray cement landscapes by introducing life-giving veins in the form of fountains.

Even more than city-dwellers, country people experience the power of water to save life but also to threaten it.

The symbolism of the baptismal water is located within that kind of experience. The liturgy of the word (Ex 14:15 to 15:1) speaks of the power of water to endanger or crush life, while the baptismal ritual makes the life-rescuing power of water the keynote of thanksgiving.

Food—Meal

Life must be sustained; it requires food and drink. Without food, life becomes impossible for the individual, but life also becomes impossible for a community unless it has its meal. Both the individual and the social aspects of food or meal find expression in the Eucharist. The "new" life of the Christian requires a "new" food. The community that has been born anew in the waters of baptism shares in the banquet of the new Passover Lamb.

Hans Hollerweger and Rudolf Schwarzenberger

Advice and Suggestions for the Conduct of the Celebration

The manner in which the Easter Vigil is to be celebrated according to the Sacramentary cannot in fact be followed in every parish. But, as even the Sacramentary allows, there are many ways in which the ritual can be adapted to varying situations. The adaptations may have to do with available space or with singers and musicians no less than with the explanation of the content of the liturgy or the active participation of the congregation.

In making the following suggestions, we presuppose that the rubrics of the Sacramentary are known.

THE SERVICE OF LIGHT

The Easter Fire

Where Are the People to Assemble?

The Sacramentary provides for the congregation gathering around the *fire*. There is no difficulty with this in smaller communities, and there the rubric should be followed. But it has become customary almost everywhere for the people to assemble *in the church* and for only the priest (with his assistants) and the servers to go to the spot where the Easter fire has been lit. The bad weather frequently encountered at this time of year (making the lighting of candles a problem outdoors) and the crush at the door of the church are justification for this custom. A future edition of the Sacramentary should take this new situation into account. But at least a group (parish council, some young people, the choir) should be invited to gather at the Easter fire; this will lend some solemnity to the ritual conducted there.

Introduction

The Sacramentary provides for an introduction to the service and even offers a model of it. If the congregation has not assembled at the fire, then of course it makes little sense to give the introduction there. One solution would be to have a lector read this introduction inside the church, using a written form (a flashlight would have to be used).

Texts: Sacramentary. The introduction must not be too long; there should be some moments of silence before the first "Christ our light!"

Fire

For the success of the ceremony there must be *darkness* in and around the church. The faithful are holding their candles (with some form of guard to catch the drops of wax). We should bear in mind here that signs "speak" only if they are not "second-best substitutes" for the real thing.

A *bonfire* is a fascinating sight, often more so to city people who see a bonfire but rarely, than to country folk. Only in exceptional cases, therefore—bad weather, for example—should the fire be dispensed with entirely and the ceremony conducted entirely inside the church (as in Sacramentary, no. 13).

Wherever possible, the bonfire should be a sizable one. A few sticks with gasoline on them have no symbolic power. A tiny fire in a tin can (no accidents please!) on the church steps, close to a heavily traveled and brightly lit street is really nonsensical. From the outset the fire should look like a fire! The best thing is to let the young people or the older servers build the fire.

As far as possible, the bonfire should be built close to the main door of the church so that its light may fill the church itself. When is the fire to be lit? If the congregation has gathered around the fire, then it is proper to set it going when the priest begins the service. If, however, the congregation assembles inside the church, then the fire should already be lit as they pass by on their way in, so that they may at least have this close experience of it.

If for the reasons given earlier the blessing of the fire must be shifted inside the church (Sacramentary, no. 13), the priest and his assistants might gather at the "holy sepulcher" (if there is one). The faithful should turn at their places and look toward the priest. The burning fire at the sepulcher is blessed and the Easter candle is lit from it (such a ceremony resembles that found in the Orthodox liturgy at Jerusalem).

After the blessing of the fire (no. 9), the *Easter candle* is lit. This is best done with a taper. The taper can then be used to light the coals in the censer. Taking pieces of charcoal from the fire can be a complicated process and usually does not have the hoped-for effect.

The Easter candle should be beautifully crafted and worthy of the song of praise that it occasions. One point, moreover, should be quite clear: there must be a new, full-sized candle each year. A candle that becomes smaller year by year and is used until it burns out is utterly incompatible with the meaning attached to the Easter candle!

The decoration of the candle may vary. It can be "decorated" in accordance with the suggestion in no. 10 of the rubrics, or may be adorned with a garland of flowers or other form of decoration. In any case, it should be a worthy image of the risen Lord.

Marking of the Easter Candle

Before the Easter candle is lit, "it may seem appropriate to stress the dignity and significance of the Easter candle with other symbolic rites" (no. 10). Since the Easter candle serves as an eloquent liturgical symbol not only during the Vigil and the Easter season but on various occasions throughout the entire year (baptisms, funerals), it is appropriate that its meaning be spelled out at the time when it is blessed. The Sacramentary suggests one way of doing this. The manner chosen for bringing out this meaning will suggest how the candle is to be decorated.

The short prayer at the lighting of the candle (no. 12) should be spoken in any case. The preceding prayers connected with the tracing of the cross and the year and with the insertion of the grains of incense will be used only where the candle itself has been suitably prepared and marked.

Incense is placed in the censer before the procession begins.

Entrance into the Church

The Order of Procession

The censer-bearer leads, followed by the deacon (priest) with the Easter candle. Even if a cantor is to sing the Easter Proclamation, it is appropriate that the deacon (or priest) carry the Easter candle. The deacon is followed by the servers, with the celebrant and his assistants bringing up the rear.

If the people have assembled around the fire, then they now follow the Easter candle, the servers, and the priest into the church. In this situation the rubrics call for "Christ our light!" to be sung for the first time at the fire; the second stop is at the door of the church, and the third at the altar. The same procedure can be followed even if there is only a small group of the faithful around the fire.

If the faithful are assembled only in the church, then the first singing of the "Christ our light!" will be at the church door (or at the "holy sepulcher"), the second at about the middle of the church, and the third at the altar.

Christ our Light!

The use of the Latin *Lumen Christi* is preferable here. It should be sung with a loud voice so as to call forth as spontaneous an answer as possible. The use of successively higher tones in the triple singing of the words is appropriate, but should not be tried at the cost of spontaneity. Kneeling after the *Deo gratias* or "Thanks be to God" is no longer prescribed and ought to be omitted, since it makes the procedure needlessly complicated.

Lighting of the Candles

The lighting of the candles by groups (priest, servers, people) is no longer prescribed; the effect of the single flame in the dark church is thereby intensified. After the second "Christ our light!" (before the third and the placing of the Easter candle on its stand) priest and servers light their candles, and the servers then light the candles of the congregation. Candles are also to be lit at the twelve crosses on the walls of a consecrated church; that is how the rubric is to be understood which says: "Then the lights in the church are put on" (no. 15, end).

The Easter Proclamation

Preparation

While the servers are lighting the candles of the congregation the actions indicated in no. 16 are performed: the priest goes to his chair; the deacon places the Easter candle on its stand; incense is placed in the censer; the deacon (but not a substitute cantor) asks for a blessing.

The spot and stand where the Easter candle is placed should be decorated. The artists of the early Church produced marvelous *Easter candle stands* that are still used today. It might well be worthwhile once more to commission that kind of Easter candle stand for the church; this stand, with the Easter candle on it, is after all to remain by the baptismal font throughout the rest of the year (after Pentecost) and is to be placed by the coffin or the altar, with the candle lit, at funerals.

If the *book* is not to be held by a server during the singing of the Easter proclamation, then it should be placed on a lectern near the Easter candle.

The Singing

Even if the candles of the congregation have not yet all been lit, the Easter Proclamation (Exsultet) is to begin *immediately* after the preparations have been completed. A lengthy pause at this point might easily be felt as a time of needless waiting; an immediate start, on the other hand, is suitable as an expression of joy. That all should stand during the Proclamation is so obvious that it really need not have been stated in the rubrics.

Extinguish the Candles?

The Sacramentary provides that after the Proclamation the candles should be put aside and lit again only when the time comes for the renewal of baptismal promises. Is the symbolic force of the lit candles diminished when these are extinguished after the Proclamation? This opinion is voiced now and then but it is not generally felt to be valid. Practical difficulties such as arise in a parish community suggest that the candles are best extinguished until the renewal of baptismal promises. The symbolism of light is, after all, continued by the still burning Easter candle. If the candles of the congregation are to be kept lit for a long period, the celebration of the Eucharist would be the appropriate time.

The effectiveness of the service of light is due to the symbolic power of light, which in this case is underscored by a straightforward singing of the Proclamation. There is no need to heighten the solemnity in any way.

We must bear in mind that the Easter Vigil is to be a "night of vigil for the Lord." The readings form the heart of the vigil celebration. The meaning of the readings will be grasped in sufficient depth only if the necessary effort has been expended on interior preparation and on the externals of the ritual. If the manner of reading is dictated by the pressure of time, the liturgy of the word will become not only meaningless, but boring and ineffective. The liturgy of the word too is to be a "celebration"; the element of singing will do more than anything else to create such an atmosphere.

Readings

Overview

Old Testament readings:

1. Gen. 1:1 to 2:2 or 1:1, 26–31a (Creation)
2. Gen 22:1–18 or 22:1–2, 9a, 10–13, 15–18 (Abraham's sacrifice)
3. Ex 14:15 to 15:1 (Crossing of the Red Sea)
4. Is 54:5–14 (The new Jerusalem)
5. Is 55:1–11 (God's offer of salvation)
6. Bar 3:9–15, 3:32 to 4:4 (The fountain of wisdom)
7. Ezek 36:16–17a, 18–28 (The new heart and the new spirit)

New Testament readings:

Epistle: Rom 6:3–11 (Dead and risen with Christ)
Gospel: A. Mt 28:1–10 (The Easter message)
      B. Mk 16:1–8
      C. Lk 24:1–12

Selection

The use of only three Old Testament readings in most

churches is the absolute minimum that is permitted. Since the reading about the crossing of the Red Sea must always be used, there are only two further readings to be selected (where the rule of the minimum is being adopted). It makes sense to read the hymn to creation (Gen 1) at every Easter Vigil celebration. The choice of a third reading from among the remaining five will depend on the homily and on the desirability of variation.

Explanation

Lent provides the best opportunity for explaining the readings of the Vigil. If on the Sundays of Lent the meaning of one or other of the Vigil readings is explained in greater detail than would be possible during the Vigil itself, the congregation will derive significantly greater profit from the liturgy of the word during the nocturnal Easter service. (Cf. above, "Importance and Overview," at the beginning of Part II of this book.)

There are three opportunities for explaining the readings during the Vigil celebration itself:

First, the brief *address of the celebrant* to the congregation at the beginning of the liturgy of the word. The words of the priest at this point are intended to stimulate the congregation to listen attentively to the readings, but it is legitimate to state briefly the main threads that run through the readings. The celebrant can return to these in his homily.

Second, *texts for a commentator* before each reading. Not as an alternative to the celebrant's short opening address, but as a complement to it, short commentaries may be read that explain each successive reading. This type of introduction is not meant to be an exegetical explanation, but a short indication of why it is this and not some other reading that conveys God's word to the community on this particular night. The "commentary" should not summarize the coming passage or blunt its impact. It should moreover be spoken by someone other than the reader of the scripture text itself. The commentaries should be carefully worded and correlated among themselves. (For models cf. the Appendix to this book.)

Third, the celebrant's *homily*. Here it will be possible to develop one or another theme from the readings, but hardly feasible to go into the Old Testament readings in a concrete and comprehensive way.

As a general rule, an explanation of the readings in some form or other is indispensable if the congregation is to give them the attention needed and if they are to be seen as relevant to the present.

The significance and importance of the readings will also be conveyed if they are well read. The singing of the readings will help to the same end. The active participation of the congregation will be helped if there is a different reader for each reading.

Intermediate Songs
The impact of the liturgy of the word will depend largely on the intermediate songs.

One of the best methods is the use of *responsorial psalms*, because they sum up the content of the readings in a meditative form and because they allow the active participation of the congregation. (Cf. below, pp. 123–24 for a selection of responsorial psalms.)

Gloria
The Gloria was, historically, an Easter song of praise. This is one of the reasons why the liturgical reformers were unwilling to omit it from the Vigil service. The repeated use of it throughout the year has admittedly blurred its paschal character in the minds of the people. Together with the prayer of the day (opening prayer), the Gloria is meant to mark the transition from the Old Testament to the New. In the Sacramentary (no. 31), its

importance is underscored by the lighting of the altar candles and the ringing of the church bells.

Given its function, the Gloria should be performed in a festive manner: singing by congregation and choir, with accompaniment if possible by organ and other instruments. If at all possible, the opening prayer which follows upon the Gloria is to be sung and not merely read.

The separation of the Old Testament readings from the New by the Gloria and the opening prayer is unusual and not fully convincing. If the subsequent Alleluia is sung in a festive mode (and only then), it is advisable to omit the Gloria and opening prayer. The decisive reason for this is that it is not easy to have two climactic moments (Gloria and Alleluia) follow so closely on one another, separated only by an opening prayer and a reading.

Moreover, is not the Alleluia the authentic song of the Easter Vigil?

Alleluia and Gospel
After the reading all stand for the Alleluia and remain standing until the end of the gospel.

The Alleluia can be sung in a relatively simple form. In the simple form, which is generally to be preferred, one of the Alleluias in *Worship II* 362 or 531 may be used. (Cf. below, pp. 125–26.)

In the more solemn form, the Alleluia is combined with elements of the old resurrection procession of the congregations; the Alleluia is then intoned at the "holy sepulcher."

After the New Testament reading, the celebrant and servers go to the "sepulcher." There the celebrant puts incense into the censer. The servers take the candles that are intended for the altar and have been made ready in advance. Then the celebrant intones the Alleluia in the usual way. After the Alleluia, the verses of Psalm 118 or an Easter song (e.g., "Jesus Christ is Risen Today") is sung in a festive manner (e.g., accompanied by wind instruments). Priest and servers go in procession to the altar. The deacon (priest) takes with him the book of gospels from which he will read the Easter gospel at the pulpit. Then the servers place their candles on the altar.

It is also quite possible to have the procession accompanied by the singing of the choir and by instrumental music, and to have an Easter song sung after the gospel as an immediate response of the congregation to the Easter message.

After the gospel (and Easter song) comes the *homily*, which should amount to a short personal profession of the Easter faith. This gives the liturgy a needed personal note which nothing can replace and which ought to be present even in the Easter Vigil. As a rule, the homily should be only a few minutes long.

Like the rest of the Vigil celebration, the liturgy of the word is meant not only to communicate truths but also to foster an experience of the Easter message. The words of scripture are simple, but they are repeated and meditated on and celebrated in song. Only thus will the length of the Vigil service (the object of so many complaints) cease to be a stumbling block; only then will the joy of Easter fill the hearts of the congregation.

THE CELEBRATION OF BAPTISM

Whenever possible, a baptism should be administered during the Easter Vigil. Especially in smaller communities, the Easter Vigil should be the first time after Ash Wednesday that baptism is administered. The ideal thing, of course, would be to have an adult baptism that is directly followed by confirmation by the priest; this would enable the community to experience the successive stages of Christian initiation.

Blessing of the Baptismal Water

The *blessing* of the water takes place at the font. But if the font is not visible to the congregation, a suitable vessel for the baptismal water should be placed in the sanctuary. In any case, the font is to be decorated. If it is customary for the faithful to take some of the consecrated water home with them, suitable preparation must be made. There is no need to distinguish between holy water and baptismal water.

If no one is to be baptized and the water alone (and not the font) is to be blessed, the litany of the saints is omitted. The blessing of the font and baptismal water is then replaced by the simple blessing of water (Sacramentary, no. 45).

The short *introduction* provided in the Sacramentary (no. 38) can most suitably be joined to the homily as its conclusion. The priest should mention the names of those to be baptized. A separate introduction only lengthens the celebration and may even be felt to be a duplication.

The order of *procession* to the place of baptism is as follows: Easter candle; candidates for baptism with their parents, godparents, and relatives; servers, and priest.

The *litany of the saints*, during which all are to stand if this is feasible, can be begun during the procession. In order to avoid disagreeable surprises, the various responses to the invocations should be sung in a mode familiar to the congregation.

The *prayer for the blessing* of the baptismal water is first and foremost one of praise of God's saving acts; only then does it turn to petition. For this reason it should be sung. The Easter candle, symbol of Christ, is lowered into the water and kept there for a moment. Such symbolic actions as this should be highly valued.

The formula for the blessing of the baptismal water is

rich in anamnetic elements. This repetition of the message already heard during the liturgy of the word, but a repetition that now takes the form of praise, is a distinct plus in the new liturgy, for it lends a thematic unity to the entire celebration. But if in a given community the repetition is felt to be rather a source of unrest, one might turn instead to the prayers of blessing in the ritual for baptism.

An acclamation by the people (Sacramentary, no. 43) closes this part of the ceremony. (For some acclamations cf. p. 126.)

Baptism
The *baptism* follows upon the acclamation and involves these rites: the renunciation, the profession of faith, baptism proper, the anointing with chrism (for those baptized who are not to be confirmed), the giving of the baptismal garment, the giving of the candle, and confirmation. The ceremonies which precede these in the baptismal ritual can be anticipated during Holy Saturday or just before the Easter Vigil either at home or in the church.

It is in keeping with the heavy responsibility laid on parents and godparents that they should make the baptismal promises in the presence of the assembled community. Unfortunately the renewal of baptismal promises by the entire commuity during the Vigil is notably separated in time from the promises made by the parents and godparents. In the introduction to the community's renewal, the celebrant should clearly mark the connection with the promises made at each new baptism; he should emphasize the responsibility which the entire community has for its nonadult members and especially for those who have been baptized during the Vigil itself. For this reason, too, the baptismal group (parents, godparents, and children) should be kept up front in sight of the community until the community itself renews its baptismal promises; only after the sprinkling of the congregation with the blessed water should the baptismal group be taken back to its place among the rest of the people.

Renewal of Baptismal Promises
After the baptism, at the time when the candle is given to the parents or to the newly baptized themselves if they be adults, the servers should light the candles of the congregation. If there is no baptism, this lighting takes place immediately after the blessing of the font or the blessing of holy water. If this lighting of candles takes a somewhat lengthy period of time, a suitable song (of praise) by the choir or an instrumental piece may be introduced to fill the time.

If the faithful have not been already standing for the litany of the saints and the blessing of the font (and this standing should not be required since the ceremony is a lengthy one), they stand now for the renewal of their baptismal promises.

There is no reason why the responses to the renunciation and the profession of faith should be different from those in the Sacramentary (no. 46). The form "I do" (I renounce, I believe) is the same as in the baptismal ritual.

The *sprinkling* with the water is done either from the font or from the altar, or else the priest walks down the aisle while doing it.

During the sprinkling a song related to baptism is sung. (Cf. below, p. 126.)

During this song the newly baptized are led to their places in the congregation.

If the blessing of the water has not taken place at the font, the servers carry the vessel of baptismal water to the font. If only holy water has been blessed at the altar, it is brought to its usual place (Sacramentary, no. 48).

In order to heighten the significance of the baptismal water (or holy water), the vessel may be left standing in front of the altar. It is then incensed during the solemn Mass of Easter and then removed during evening service (Vespers, for example) on Easter day.

Intercessions

After the solemn baptismal promises and the long prayer service these may seem almost superfluous.

If new members have been brought into the community, the ancient Christian "prayer of the faithful" should not be omitted. This is also the place for introducing topical, but general concerns. The Easter Vigil should not be just a beautiful celebration; present needs must also have their place in it.

MASS

The Eucharist is the joyous festive meal of which Paul speaks in 1 Corinthians (5:8). This spirit of festive joy should permeate the celebration, not so much in the form of outward display as in the way in which priest and people conduct the celebration.

One means of emphasizing the Eucharist as high point of the Vigil is to not extinguish the *candles* of the faithful after the baptismal promises, but to keep them burning until the end of the Eucharistic prayer.

The newly baptized should bring the *bread and wine* to the altar, with the parents and godparents doing it in place of infants. A festive Easter song would provide an appropriate accompaniment. If possible, the choir should do the singing, thus giving the congregation an opportunity for meditation.

The altar should be prepared in the usual way. If a *blessing of food* is customary, small groups may bring this up at the offertory and place it on a table in the sanctuary.

If possible, all of the faithful should be given the opportunity to receive communion in both forms. It is recommended that during the communion procession a psalm or hymn with an Alleluia refrain be sung. This will help the congregation to think of this communion as an Easter banquet of joy.

A most appropriate *song of thanksgiving* after communion is either "Alleluia! Alleluia! Praise the Lord" or "Christ the Lord Is Risen Today" (*ICEL Resource Collection* 64, 70).

The *blessing of food*, if there is one, comes after the concluding prayer.

Easter dinner at which the blessed food is eaten should bring everyone together in a spirit of Easter joy. Just before the blessing of the food the celebrant can voice this thought together with his wishes for a blessed Easter.

The celebration of the Easter Vigil ends with the *final blessing*, which should be sung.

As the people leave the church, the church bells may be rung. If they have already been rung during the thanksgiving or recessional hymn, the ringing should continue until the congregation has left the church.

The faithful may carry their candles to the graves of their relatives (assuming that the cemetery is located at the church) and then take them home.

Hubert Dopf

Importance and Execution of Song and Music During the Easter Vigil

The Easter Vigil is, without qualification, the *high point of the liturgical year*. What is true, therefore, of every liturgical celebration will be all the more true of the Easter Vigil, namely, that sacred music "forms a necessary or integral part of the solemn liturgy" and that "liturgical worship is given a more noble form when the divine offices are celebrated solemnly in song."[1] Consequently, the norm for the celebration of Easter is that "in a very special way, the sacred rites of Holy Week should be given due solemnity, since these lead the faithful to the center of the liturgical year and of the liturgy itself through the celebration of the Paschal Mystery."[2]

Since church musicians play a very important role in creating and assuring this atmosphere of solemnity, they have a major responsibility. It will depend largely on them whether the Easter Vigil truly becomes a festive celebration. It is important, therefore, that their planning be timely and comprehensive.

Timely
The great amount of work to be done for the Vigil requires that preparation be started in good time. After Christmas, at the latest, all those involved (parish priests, liturgy committee, conductor of the choir, cantor) should be informed about how the Easter triduum

will be celebrated. Full use must be made of the time between Christmas and Easter if the extensive work to be done is to be completed.

Comprehensive

Planning must include not only the songs, responses, choral pieces and so on, but also the balanced use of the various musical talents available (congregation, cantor, schola, choir, instrumentalists). During the Easter Vigil, use should be made of every possible resource.

A *quartet* (or more) *of wind instruments* can make an exceptional contribution to the festive character of the occasion; advantage should be taken of this possibility. For example, whenever the congregation sings its Easter songs, it can be accompanied by wind instruments. Straight instrumental music on the winds is also possible; for example, during the procession with the gifts or when it takes a little time to go from sanctuary to font. On such occasions, however, the usual processional marches would be out of place; short interludes would be appropriate. Finally, the use of winds (and organ) at the end of the service will once again emphasize its festive character.

In planning the use of all available musical resources, we must not however, forget to allow for a peaceful, recollected listening on the part of those in attendance. There must be no well-intentioned but disorganized accumulation of musical pieces that crowd in on one another or that become an end in themselves instead of being at the service of the solemn liturgy.

A word on the *placement of the choir*: it may be necessary to have the choir do its singing near the organ and therefore, in some cases, in the choir loft. But consideration should be given to the possibility of having the choir join in the celebration of the Easter Vigil and make its contribution to it from a place near the altar. If that is done, the choir should not of course be allowed to be a distraction, nor should the almost inevitable movements of the choir director be allowed to disturb the peace and recollection of the congregation.

With regard to *singing by the congregation* one principle must be unconditionally observed: the liturgies of the Easter triduum are not a time for trying out new songs. This means that songs and responses must have been learned already, perhaps during Lent or during the Easter season of the previous year. Nor should we forget that many people come for the Easter Vigil who do not attend church regularly. Furthermore, if groups of children or young people are to provide a nucleus for congregational singing, they must be trained in advance!

The music director should not neglect to keep a careful diary for the triduum, in which he not only lists the songs, choral pieces, and so on, but also notes any important technical directives for the conduct of the service. Immediately after each service he should indicate in this diary whatever, for example, may have turned out to be obtrusive or disturbing in this year's service and might therefore be improved on next year. Such technical directives and notes make next year's planning easier and will eliminate in advance numerous faults.

Under the following headings, various musical suggestions are made for the individual parts of the Easter Vigil.

THE SERVICE OF LIGHT
When it is possible to light the new fire close to the door of the church so that the gleam of the flames can be seen even inside the church, the result is a welcome contrast: the peaceful light of the Easter candle stands out against the flickering flames. Then the cry "Christ our light!" breaks into the stillness. These are the first words to be sung no matter where and in what manner the blessing of the fire is done.

In my opinion, the Latin *Lumen Christi* should be kept because from a musical point of view it is, so to speak, more single-minded; that is, the first two syllables "Lu-men" prepare the way for the key syllable "*Chri-*(sti)," with the final syllable, "-sti," putting an organic end to the cry. In the singing of the English "Christ our light," on the other hand, the emphasis is distributed between "Christ" and "light."

The triple singing on a successively higher note intensifies the effect. But care must be taken not to begin the acclamation the first time on too low a note for fear of otherwise being unable to reach the third and highest note! The first acclamation, too, should ring out strong and intense.

EXSULTET
It is important that there be no period of empty waiting after the third acclamation; rather, the chanting of the Exsultet should begin as soon as the ministers have reached their places in the sanctuary, and the Easter candle has been placed in its stand.

The musical version of the Exsultet that is found in the Sacramentary will normally be used. It is evidently better to have a cantor sing the Exsultet well than to have a priest or deacon do only a mediocre job with it or even sing it badly. If a cantor does sing it, certain passages are omitted.

A number of suggestions have been made for acclamations by the congregation during the course of the Exsultet. And in fact the Sacramentary itself says that "the conferences of bishops may also adapt the text by inserting acclamations for the people" (Rubrics, no. 17). From a musical point of view there is absolutely no need for such acclamations; in fact, they would rather disturb the solemn flow of this unique song. True enough, the Exsultet was probably put together out of originally separate parts, but the end result was a single whole which was to be sung by a deacon as a solemn hymn of praise. Nowhere in the entire Roman liturgy is there another composition of such dimensions and power. This unified composition should not be broken up. The introduction of acclamations would only disturb the inner peace of the listeners as they allow the song to work its emotional effect on them. The listeners, too, after all, should allow themselves to be caught up in the fervor and in what I might almost call the "cosmic devotion" that mark this song. If no singer is available who can tackle the Exsultet in its entirety, the short version may always be used.

LITURGY OF THE WORD

The series of readings is broken up by responsorial psalms. The number and choice of readings must be decided on in advance so that these songs can be planned and practiced. There is a wide range of possibilities here.

Cantor and Congregation

The cantor and congregation can sing responses and psalm verses. This presupposes that the community must be already accustomed to responsorial singing. The Easter Vigil should not be their first introduction to it. Nothing detracts more from a celebration than a wretched, poorly done psalm.

In choosing the psalms two considerations are normative: psalms assigned to the readings of the Easter Vigil should be preferred, and suitable, well-known responses should be chosen in which the congregation can join with animation. The following responses to the individual readings are included in the Lectionary:

After the second reading—Resp.: "Keep me safe, O God; you are my hope," with Psalm 16.
　　Psalm 104.
After the second readings—Resp.: "Keep me safe, O God; you are my hope," with Psalm 16.

After the third reading—Resp.: "Let us sing to the Lord; he has covered himself in glory," with Exodus 15.

After the fourth reading—Resp.: "Lord, thou hast drawn me up," with Psalm 30.

After the fifth reading—Resp.: "You will draw water joyfully from the springs of salvation," with Isaiah 12.

After the sixth reading—Resp.: "Lord, you have the words of everlasting life," with Psalm 19.

After the seventh reading—Resp.: "Like a deer that longs for running streams, my soul longs for you, my God," with Psalms 42–43.

Musical settings of these psalms are found in *The Gelineau Gradual* (GIA) and *The Cantor Book* (WLP). For additional settings, consult *The Psalm Locator* (Resource Publications).

Congregation
Instead of an antiphon along with the singing of psalm verses by the soloist, a *song* may be sung by the congregation as a response to a reading, but this should be an exception. There are various possibilities, according to the content of the scripture passage just read; for example, "Praise the Lord" (*Worship II* 229) or "Earth and All Stars" (in either the setting in *Worship II* 69 or in the *Lutheran Book of Worship* 558) might be used as a response after the creation reading. Many songs based on the psalms (or at least many stanzas from such songs) are direct responses to a given reading. Careful selection is necessary, of course. This means that a stanza or stanzas that suit the reading will be chosen, instead of singing such songs straight through.

Choir
The choir may be used for the responsorial songs. To be recommended here is some suitable polyphonic psalm or song based on a psalm, or some responsorial song set

for several voices. Choral material from older works offers items still quite usable today.

The varied use of these different possible methods can make for a heightened effect.

If possible, there should be a number of cantors. It would be appropriate, for example, that the singer of the Exsultet should not sing again during this celebration. Or several cantors may take turns after the several readings.

GLORIA

This should not be *the* musical high point of the service! During the Vigil, the Gloria is always to be intoned by the priest. If the choir is to sing the Gloria (as seems sensible), a setting should be chosen that is not too ornate. Festive, yes, but not too expansive from the musical point of view. The Gloria continues the surge of praise that reached its first high point in the Exsultet.

The New Testament reading that follows upon the Gloria should if possible be sung.

ALLELUIA

The Alleluia in its ancient form (*Worship II* 531) is to be recommended and given preference. The old custom may be followed of singing the Alleluia three times, each time beginning a full note higher, and of having the congregation repeat it after the soloist.

If the melody in *Worship II* 531 seems too difficult, then the simple Easter Alleluia (*Worship II* 362), which everyone can sing, may be used.

After the Alleluia, a soloist sings verses from Ps 118. A recommended setting is *Alleluia and Psalm for Easter* by Richard Proulx (*GIA # 1965*).

The *gospel* is to be sung in solemn fashion by a deacon or priest. This means that care must be given to the acclamation of the people. If the gospel is sung, an acclamation that is simply spoken will seem rather shabby. One possibility is to sing an Easter song, or at least the Alleluia of it, as a solemn response of the congregation.

THE CEREMONY OF BAPTISM
The *litany of the saints* should really be sung; the singing of it will take hardly any more time than the reading of it. The melody in *Worship II* 534 is preferable to the setting in the Sacramentary, no. 41. In the former, the responses of the congregation correspond to the Latin responses. Needless to say, a well-prepared choir is essential for leading the congregation.

For the *acclamation* after the Blessing of Water (Sacramentary, no. 43), only those well-known to the congregation should be used. A number of acclamations are included in the *ICEL Resource Collection*, nos. 259–266, 274, 315.

The Sacramentary provides that the *Vidi aquam*—"I saw water flowing"—be sung during the *sprinkling with the blessed water* (no. 47). Unless the congregation is quite familiar with this song, it would be safer to use some other song, appropriate for baptism, which they know well. Some suggestions: "The Water I Give" in *Liturgy in Lent* (NPM), and "Come and Let Us Drink of That New River" (*Worship II* 48). It would be worth asking whether one of these songs should be sung in parts by the choir; then the congregation could attend to the sprinkling without being distracted by having to follow a hymnal.

THE EUCHARIST
An Easter hymn sung by the congregation may serve as an accompaniment to the preparation of the gifts. Organ music (an Easter prelude) might be appropriate. But the movement of the service should not be slowed

down. The congregation should be moved to joy by the music, but the Eucharist should not be interrupted.

COMMUNION
Either responsorial singing of cantor (or choir) and congregation, or choral music alone may be used. In planning the music at this point, it should be kept in mind that most of the choir will probably be going to communion. A hymn or psalm that uses an "Alleluia" refrain should be the first choice here. For responsorial singing use Ps 118. Responses suitable for the same Psalm are *Worship II* 540.

Depending on the time needed for distributing communion, the choice of organ music alone is suitable. Other instruments (horns) may also be used.

A solemn *hymn of thanksgiving* (e.g., "Alleluia! Alleluia! Praise the Lord" or "Christ the Lord Is Risen Today" in *ICEL Resource Collection* 64, 70) should end the communion service. But keep in mind that toward the end of this lengthy nocturnal liturgy, the celebration should move along expeditiously.

The solemn *final blessing* should be sung, provided here again that the responses are familiar to the congregation and come spontaneously. Nothing so disrupts a joyous festive close as a final blessing that is timorously sung or poorly answered. The "Thanks be to God, alleluia, alleluia" must ring out sure and strong. A closing song by the congregation is not needed here; festive organ music or horns provide a better ending. The ringing of the church bells as the congregation leaves also underscores the uniqueness of this nocturnal celebration.

The celebration of the Easter Vigil now has a secure place among believers in the Christian community. As far as the music for the Vigil is concerned, however, the situation is unsatisfactory. For some time yet we shall have to settle for solutions that are not entirely satisfying. For this reason church musicians and those responsible for the liturgy will have to do their careful and conscientious best so that the desired form may at last emerge from the many available resources and experiments.

NOTES

1. Vatican II, *Constitution on the Sacred Liturgy*, nos. 112 and 113, in A. Flannery (ed.), *Vatican II: The Conciliar and Postconciliar Documents* (Collegeville, Minn., 1975), pp. 31–32.

2. Sacred Congregation of Rites, Instruction *Musicam sacram* on Music in the Liturgy (March 5, 1967), no. 44, in Flannery, p. 91.

IV. Extension of the Easter Celebration to Parish and Family

Hans Hollerweger

Children's Celebration on Holy Saturday

The development of special liturgies for children as part of the postconciliar liturgical reform has led to the celebration in recent years of special children's liturgies even during the Easter triduum. These have been quite successful. It is, of course, not unconditionally necessary that every liturgy should in principle have a duplicate geared to children (we do not follow such a principle in secular life). Yet there are certainly good reasons which justify special liturgies for children in certain circumstances; for example, if the regular celebration starts in the evening, or if the liturgy for adults is quite long.

For *Holy Thursday* and *Good Friday* the content and form of the celebrations is largely determined by the character of the liturgy itself. That is, on Holy Thursday a Mass is celebrated in a form intended for children, while on Good Friday there is a passion celebration that makes use of the way of the cross and the veneration of the cross. The situation is different when it comes to a liturgy for children on *Holy Saturday*. The Vigil celebration is under no circumstances to be moved forward to the afternoon. The celebration of Easter takes place during the night and is not to begin before nightfall (Sacramentary: Rubrics, no. 3). This regulation holds even for children. Under no circumstances should they be given the impression that what adults will be celebrating during the night, the children may now celebrate on the previous afternoon. This would be incompatible with the meaning of the three days of the triduum, in which Holy Saturday is the day of the Lord's repose in the tomb. This is why the Sacramentary says: "On Holy Saturday the Church waits at the Lord's tomb, meditating on his suffering and death. The altar is left bare, and the sacrifice of the Mass is not celebrated. Only after the solemn vigil during the night, held in anticipation of the resurrection, does the Easter celebration begin, with a spirit of joy that overflows into the following period of fifty days" (Sacramentary: Introduction under "Holy Saturday").

If the children are able without difficulty to attend the Vigil celebration, then there should be no special liturgy for them. In addition, Easter Sunday itself provides the opportunity for a children's liturgy in which they can express their joy. If, however, a children's celebration is held on Holy Saturday, it can only take the form of a period spent at the tomb of Jesus and a preparation for the Easter Vigil.

What follows is a model for a children's liturgy on Holy Saturday in which the principles just given have been observed.

ADORATION AT THE TOMB AND PREPARATION FOR THE VIGIL

Preliminaries
At the church door each child should write his or her *baptismal name* on a slip of paper. Before the litany of the saints begins, an assistant should eliminate names that are very close but not identical. The series of baptismal names that result should be arranged approximately in the order in which they appear in the litany. For many names the saint reflected in them will not be in the liturgy and must be hunted up.
Torsy, *Der grosse Heiligenkalendar* [Freiburg, 1975]).
The children may bring *flowers* to lay at the tomb. They can be instructed on this at the children's liturgy on Good Friday.

Uniting the Congregation
One group of children sings "What Wonderous Love Is
This" or "Jesus Walked This Lonesome Valley" (*Worship
II* 306 or 150). A period of silence should follow the
hymn.

Gospel
Mt 27:45–46: Jesus is crucified and buried.

The passage should be read very serenely and slowly by
an adult.

Song
"Were You There" (American spiritual) or a setting of
the "Lamb of God."

Tableau Based on Mt 27:62–66
"The chief priests ask that the tomb be guarded."

The scene is played by boys. Costumes may be used; if
so, they should be simple.

Pilate sits on a stool that is placed there before the beginning of the celebration.

Pilate: I am Pilate. What I have written remains written: Jesus of Nazareth, King of the Jews. I gave the
corpse to Joseph of Arimathea for burial. I hope that
peace will now return at last. A great stone has been
set before the tomb, and no one can move it. Nothing
more can happen.

(About five boys representing chief priests and
Pharisees come before Pilate.)

First Pharisee: Pilate, you are our ruler. Allow us to address you. We recall that when this Jesus was still
alive he said: after three days I shall be raised up.
All the Pharisees: Yes, that is what he told people: after
three days I shall be raised up.
First Pharisee: Therefore give orders that the tomb
should be closely guarded until the third day.

Pilate: But Jesus is dead and buried. Why do you want a guard?

Second Pharisee: Some of his disciples may come, steal the body, and tell the people: He has risen from the dead.

All the Pharisees: Then the situation would be worse than before.

Pilate: If you think so, you shall have a guard from among my soldiers.

Third Pharisee: Thank you, Pilate, for granting our request.

Pilate: Go and secure the grave as fully as possible.

Fourth Pharisee: We will seal the great stone, so that no one will be able to remove it.

Fifth Pharisee: We will have a close watch set on the tomb so that no one can steal the body of Jesus.

All the Pharisees: We will do everything to prevent anyone from deceiving us.

Pilate: Go and obtain the guards. I find the whole business laughable. Never before has anyone kept guard over a dead body in a tomb.

(Pilate leaves. The chief priests and Pharisees choose six boys as "guards"; these boys have been selected in advance and wear no costumes. These boys go with the chief priests and Pharisees to the tomb. There the "guards" remain; the chief priests and Pharisees leave.)

Homily of the Priest
The celebrant explains to the children the meaning of the Lord's repose in the tomb. At the end of his address he exhorts them to approach the tomb and lay their flowers there. The children should also be instructed to genuflect before the Blessed Sacrament.

Procession to the Tomb
During the procession to the tomb the decade of the rosary invoking "Jesus who was buried for us" should be prayed. If the procession lasts longer than the time

required for a decade, a group of flute players may provide music, or else a new decade, "Jesus who was crucified for us," may be said first.

Preparation of the Easter Candle
Explanation by the celebrant. He tells the children that this tomb is filled not with darkness but with light and that from this tomb the Easter light rises. This tomb is able to enlighten us.

Bringing of the Candles
The six "guards" bring six candles from the tomb and station themselves in the sanctuary (but not right next to the altar).

A response is sung: "The Lord is my light and my salvation" (any setting of Ps 27, perhaps the one by John Foley in *A Dwelling Place* [NALR]).

Then the (unlit) *Easter candle* is brought by some of the older children. The celebrant then tells the children that this is the candle that will be lit during the coming night. If possible, the candle is now decorated with its symbols. The celebrant explains the symbols that are thus put on the Easter candle.

The Easter candle is placed on a stand but *not* lit. The other candles are still held by the "guards" in the sanctuary.

Preparation of the Font and the Baptismal Water
The celebrant makes reference to the blessing of baptismal water and the baptism that will be administered during the coming Vigil service. The font is now to be decorated in preparation for the later ceremony.

Some children bring the *decorations* for the font (flowers, a garland). They approach the font and decorate it.

Then the priest asks two (previously designated) children to bring the *water* to be blessed and used in baptism. The children bring it and pour it into the font.

Then the children may sing "Spring of Water" (*Worship II* 535) or "We Come to You, Lord Jesus" (*ICEL* 266).

The priest urges the children to call out the patronal names that remind each of his or her own baptism. Prayers are also offered for all children who will be baptized in this water during the Vigil (or during the Easter season).

A *litany of the patron saints* of the children present is now prayed (after the manner of the litany of the saints). The priest first tells the children what their responses will be (*P/A* = Priest/All).

P/A: Lord, have mercy.
P/A: Christ, have mercy.
P/A: Lord, have mercy.
P: Holy Mary, Mother of God.
A: Pray for us.
P: Saint . . . (the children's patron saints are named).
P: All you saints of God.
A: Pray for us.
P: We poor sinners.
A: Lord, hear our prayer.
P: Sanctify this water for the baptism of your children.
A: Lord, hear our prayer.
P: Through this water grant these children a share in eternal life.
A: Lord, hear our prayer.
P: Help us to live as baptized Christians.
A: Lord, hear our prayer.
P: Jesus, Son of the living God.
A: Lord, hear our prayer.
P: Christ, hear us.
A: Christ, hear us.
P: Lord Jesus, hear your people.
A: Lord Jesus, hear our prayer.
(The priest concludes the litany with the following prayer:)

136

May this water remind us of our baptism. May it unite us in Easter joy with all the children who will be baptized during this night of Easter and with all who have been reborn of water and the Holy Spirit for everlasting life.

Preparation of the Altar

The celebrant asks that the altar now be prepared for the Easter Vigil.

Two children bring the *altarcloth* and spread it on the altar. As they do, they say aloud: "We cover the table for the Easter meal that Jesus will celebrate with us."

Two more children bring a *crucifix* and place it on the altar. As they do, they say: "We bring the cross. Jesus died on a cross for us."

The six "guards" place their candles near the altar (or on it). As they do, they say: "We bring the light. Christ is the light of the world."

Some children bring *flowers*, saying: "We bring flowers. We are glad that Easter has come."

Joyous music is played on the flute (or the organ).

Conclusion of the Celebration

The Our Father is said together. Then the celebrant extends his hands over the children and prays: "Lord, our God, may your rich blessing descend on these children and all here present. They are waiting for the resurrection of your Son. Grant them Easter joy. We ask this through Christ, our Lord. Amen."

Closing Song

"Sing to the Mountains" (*Earthen Vessels*) or another joyful hymn. (Hymns used throughout this celebration should not contain "Alleluias.")

Hans Hollerweger

Is Easter Sunday Being Neglected?
Two Suggestions

A distinction is called for here. Easter Sunday begins
with the celebration of the Easter Vigil and ends on
Easter Sunday evening (therefore the Sacramentary has
the heading "Easter Sunday" *before* that of "Easter
Vigil"). There can therefore be no question of claiming
that the new order for the Easter triduum fails to do
justice to Easter Sunday. The problem, insofar as there
is one, is at a different level. Only in exceptional cases is
the Vigil liturgy celebrated in the early morning of
Easter or at midnight of Holy Saturday. As a rule it is
celebrated during the evening of Holy Saturday. Those,
however, who join in the celebration of the Vigil (even
if it be held the previous evening) have already celebrated Easter Sunday and are not obliged to attend
another liturgy on Easter day. In addition, the Vigil is
celebrated with great solemnity. Does not all this mean
that the festive liturgy on Easter Sunday is somewhat
neglected?

These two celebrations should not, of course, be played
off against one another. On the whole, the celebration
of Easter has gained depth and effectiveness through
the introduction of the Easter Vigil. But a justifiable
question remains: Is anything *special* done on Easter
Sunday to bring home its meaning to those who were
unable to celebrate the Vigil? What provision is made
for those who want to make Easter Sunday a festive
occasion?

If the Vigil liturgy is held at midnight or in the early morning, it will certainly detract from the celebration during the day. In this case is not some *celebration on Easter evening* all the more necessary in order that Easter day too may be experienced as a day of celebration?

The following suggestions are meant as stimuli that are usable, for the most part, only in areas that have kept the relevant traditional customs.

EASTER PROCESSION ON EASTER SUNDAY

When the Easter Vigil was introduced, the Easter procession *before* the Vigil was prohibited. In the early years of the reform an effort was made to link the procession with the Vigil. But such a candlelight procession, when attached to the Vigil liturgy, only further lengthened an already long service and gave the impression, moreover, of a catacomb procession rather than a festive one. The procession therefore no longer had a determinate place and liturgical context and disappeared. On the other hand, laments are still frequently heard about the absence of the old "ressurrection celebration" which consisted almost entirely of a procession in the church or around the church or through the locality.

Since Holy Saturday no longer provides a place for such a procession, it can, if revived, be meaningfully celebrated only on Easter Sunday. It could, for example, be held in connection with the High Mass, with the most appropriate time for it being just before this Mass. The starting point for the procession would be the altar or, if there is one, a "holy sepulcher." If the latter is there, then of course the figure of Christ reposing in the tomb would have to be covered or removed (after the Vigil, at the latest); a statue of the risen Jesus would be placed in front of the tomb and given festive lighting.

The procession could be introduced by the singing of the triple Alleluia (on successive higher tones) and the acclamation "Christ is risen" (Alleluia and acclamation intoned by the priest). The statue of the risen Jesus would be carried in the procession, and where customary, the instruments of the passion as well. The procession would also provide an opportunity for the children, usually not present at the Vigil service, to play a part in the celebration of Easter. The procession should be a festive one, as used to be customary in rural areas: the church bells rung, banners carried, orchestra playing, the people singing and praying.

It would be appropriate to include the cemetery on the route of the procession, provided nothing smacking of a liturgy of the dead be allowed to develop. Since the custom of carrying candles from the Vigil to the cemetery has already sprung up in many places, the visit to the cemetery during an Easter procession would sit well. A stop could be made at the cemetery, with the singing of the Easter gospel and the offering of intercessions. But the visit to the cemetery should not be allowed to give an exclusive coloring to the procession, so that any appearance of a liturgy of the dead may be avoided.

There is no reason for taking the Eucharist in the procession. It is better to reserve this special trait to the Corpus Christi procession. The statue of the risen Jesus serves adequately as a focal point for the procession.

After the procession reenters the Church, the Mass is celebrated. It may begin in the usual manner with the entrance song or, because of the foregoing procession, with the readings.

In areas where the "resurrection celebration" had taken the form of an Easter procession and had had a strong hold on the popular mind, the connecting of the solemn Mass with a procession could give the old custom a new importance and root it more deeply in the consciousness of the people, without detracting from the Vigil celebration.

Vespers on Easter Sunday marks the liturgical close of the Easter triduum. This principle should not be allowed to be a dead letter but rather should be applied in the parish community.

In areas where it has been traditional, the festive celebration of Easter Vespers is taken for granted.

If Vespers need to be introduced anew, it is best to sing only a few parts, for instance, the hymn, the New Testament Canticle, and the Canticle of Mary. Musical settings are found in the *ICEL Resource Collection* 351–353, 115, 258.

At the Canticle of Mary (Magnificat) not only the altar but the baptismal water as well is incensed.

If the baptismal water has been blessed not in the font but at the main altar, it is now carried in procession to the font and poured into it. This is best done after the prayer of Vespers.

The final blessing can be given with the Blessed Sacrament in the usual manner, as found in Holy Communion and Worship of the Eucharist Outside of Mass.

Hans Hollerweger

Easter in the Family: Suggestions for Families

The service in the church should not be like an isolated island in the middle of a broad ocean. That which is celebrated in the church must radiate its light into the rest of life and take root in the people through being celebrated especially in the family. Conversely, it is through family celebrations that the ground is prepared for the celebration in the church. Christmas provides us with the best example of what it means for a feast to be deeply rooted in the life of the family. Were we to ask children which is the most important of all feasts, the answer would most likely be "Christmas." The Christmas tree, the crib, the many songs, the custom of giving and receiving presents, the usual greetings, and so on, have all contributed to the preeminence of this feast.

In the Eastern Churches the feast of Easter enjoys an influence comparable to that of our Christmas. There people wish one another a happy Easter with the greeting: "Christ is risen"—"Yes, he is truly risen!" A deeply experienced "sacred Easter Vigil" has caused this feast to penetrate fully into the consciousness of the Eastern Christians.

To what extent has the feast of Easter taken root in the family life and popular consciousness of Western Christians? The entire Easter celebration, beginning with Palm Sunday, has indeed created an influential set of customs (e.g., the bringing home of palms), but the feast of Easter itself has made little impression or has done so in a way that really does not get to the heart of

Easter. The blessing of food, for example, recalls the older rigorous practice of fasting which did not permit eggs to be eaten during Lent. These now reappeared on the table at Easter as gifts that had been blessed. The Easter rabbit that brings the eggs is popular with children and there is no reason for taking away the happiness this little animal brings them. The rabbit came to be thus honored at Easter because it supposedly slept with its eyes open, but even at best it is a rather poor symbol of the resurrection. It must be admitted, then, that apart from numerous local customs there are few bridges between the Easter liturgy in church and the life of household and family.

What can be done to help the Easter faith leave a deeper impress on the life of families? There is only one way: simple symbolic actions that are intelligible to all must create a link between the Easter faith as expressed in church and family life. The many symbols used in the Vigil celebration point us in one possible direction.

MEANINGFUL CUSTOMS

If customs are to exercise their function, they must, as it were, rise up from the depths of consciousness and help people to cultivate spiritual values. There is need, therefore, of a spiritual broadening of minds, especially when symbolic actions are being appropriated for the first time.

Just as the Church prepares the faithful for Easter during the forty days of Lent, so too families must prepare at home for Easter. The chief form such a preparation will take will be for the parents and children to participate with greater fervor in the liturgy and to shape the life of the family in the light of the liturgy. Preparation for Sunday Mass, an occasional reading from Scripture, a decade of the Sorrowful Mysteries of the rosary, or a way of the cross might be forms of prayer adopted by the family. Fasting should also be practiced in some of its various possible forms: the choice of less delectable meals on Friday, deliberate self-denial in regard to what is available, sharing with the needy.

This preparation reaches its climax in the celebration of *Holy Week* in church and in the home. The *palm branches* that are brought home from the Palm Sunday liturgy are a first sign of the Easter victory of Christ. The children could prepare the branches themselves and bring them to church. Usually the branches are attached to a crucifix or set in an appropriate place. The gravity of *Good Friday* should be felt in the family, with the older children gladly taking part in the fast. At about three o'clock in the afternoon a candle might be lit (beside the crucifix) and a minute of recollection observed.

On *Holy Saturday* preparation is made for the Easter Vigil. A visit to the "holy sepulcher" will make a deep impression, especially on children, and will rouse in the entire family a consciousness of waiting for the resurrection. Candles are decorated for the Vigil celebration and for the family table. The lantern to be used for bringing home the Easter flame from the church is set in order. The Easter ornament (Easter bouquet) is set in its place. The eggs are colored, and the basket containing bread, meat, and eggs is made ready for the blessing of food in the church. The container for holy water is cleansed. As all these actions are performed, their meaning can be explained to the children: the light as a sign of Christ who desires to remove all darkness and gloom from our lives; the foods from which people used to abstain throughout Lent and which are now the first foods to be eaten after the Easter Vigil as a sign that the Lord himself wants to share a meal with us; the eggs as a sign of life; the lifegiving water as a symbol of our baptism. The children can also be told why it is that we use holy water throughout the year and make the sign of the cross on ourselves with it: the water and the signing are intended to remind us that we must live as baptized persons, that is, as Christians.

If this or a similar preparation is made at home for the Easter Vigil, a sense of joyous expectation will be awakened in the children. They will want to be present at the Vigil and will have a better understanding of the symbols used in the liturgy. A special celebration for children does of course supply an opportunity for an explanation of Easter that is geared to children. But it is even better if children want to be allowed to attend the celebration for adults. What they experience in the Church during the Vigil will not strike them as strange, because they themselves have done a good deal of the preparation for it.

THE FAMILY CELEBRATION
This can take its lead from the symbols used in the nocturnal Vigil service.

Easter Light
After the Vigil, the people who had attended it should be given an opportunity to light their own candles at the Easter candle and then to take these home with them in the lantern prepared for the purpose. On arriving home they light the candle that has been set on the festive table and place the candle brought from church beside the crucifix. It would be a fine idea to leave this candle burning all through Easter Sunday.

If possible, all should go together to the cemetery after the Vigil service and there light the candles at the graves of their relatives. The children thus see how the significance of the Easter Vigil as a service of light extends to an area which they will have little other opportunity to experience in such depth.

Easter Water
After the Vigil the blessed water should be drawn from the vessel in church and taken home in a jug or decorated flask. At home the holy water font is filled anew with the newly blessed water.

Easter Dinner

The Easter banquet held in church is extended into the family by means of the festive Easter meal at home. The point is to give expression to the fact that the hope which we all need has been given to every individual and to every area of life by the resurrection of Jesus. The hope finds expression in mutual forgiveness, in the opportunity repeatedly to begin again, in the courage with which we attack our problems. A record with background music might be used to create a joyous mood during the meal.

Families clearly need guidance and instruction if they are to celebrate Easter at home as well as in the church. As at Christmas so at Easter a little family ritual can be built up: "This is how we celebrate Easter at our house!" The guidance can be given at meetings of families or of housewives or mothers. Another possibility would be to preach occasionally during Lent on the celebration of Easter in the home. Still another possibility for educating the children in the meaning of Easter would be the catechism class or the group discussion.

The purpose in all this is to help the people become more fully and deeply conscious of the greatest feast in the liturgical year. If the Easter symbols of light, water, and food are connected with ordinary life and if their expressive power is experienced within the home, they will contribute to a more comprehensive experience of the Easter message.

BLESSING AT TABLE FOR EASTER

Father: In the name of the Father and of the Son and the Holy Spirit. Amen. This is the day the Lord has made, alleluia.

All: Let us rejoice and be glad in it, alleluia.

Father: Glory be to the Father and to the Son and to the Holy Spirit.

All: As it was in the beginning, is now, and will be forever. Amen.

Father: Let us pray. Lord Jesus Christ, after your resurrection you sat at table with your disciples. We ask
you to bestow your presence on us as well. And just
as we shall be filled by the food prepared for us, so
too grant us a share in your Easter life, you who live
and reign for ever and ever.
All: Amen.

Appendix

Introductions for Use in the Easter Vigil

INTRODUCTION BEFORE THE SERVICE

Brothers and sisters! We have gathered in the *darkness* of the night because the Lord willingly entered the night of death. This night of his dying we celebrated yesterday.

Today we celebrate his *victory* over that night. The light we shall see will tell us that Christ has power to overcome all the darkness of the world and of our individual lives.

We have gathered in the *dark* because there is so much darkness in us and around us: sin, anxiety, doubt, lukewarmness, weakness. . . .

In this night that shall become as bright as the day, we will hear the message: hope is ours because of the resurrection of Jesus; we must begin anew, we must be courageous, for *in every darkness we have a light*, the risen Lord!

We meet him in this celebration in the *symbol of light*, and we cry out to him: *Lumen Christi—Christ our light!*

We meet him in his *word* and reflect on how mightily this word has acted in the history of salvation and what it intends to do in our day.

The *blessing of the baptismal water* and the *administration of baptism* will remind us of our own call to faith and will summon us to a new "Yes!"

In the *Eucharist* we will thank the Lord for his call to us and we will share in the Easter banquet which the risen Lord himself prepares for us.

GREETING AND INTRODUCTION AFTER THE EXSULTET

Brothers and sisters! With festive joy we have lit our candles from the new flame and have listened to the praises of this holiest night in the year. We have begun our Easter Vigil.

Now we want to take some time to listen quietly and meditatively to readings which will describe the great redemptive acts which God has done for his people from earliest times. After each reading let us pray silently with all our heart that God would repeat his miracles of new life in the Church of our day and that he would grant our world the power to believe and to hope for the future.

Or:

My dear people! We have begun this holiest of all nights with praise of the light that will illumine the coming hours. Let us now quietly take our seats and try to become silent within ourselves as well as in our outward behavior.

God's Word that created our world and is still shaping it seeks to make its way into our hearts and so to make the whole world new.

God's Word took human form in Christ. That Word desires to suffer and struggle at our side and thus lead us too to victory.

INTRODUCTIONS TO THE INDIVIDUAL READINGS

First Reading (Creation)
The first reading is about the "primeval night" that was filled with light by God's creative Word. We do not simply listen here to a story of a past event. We make an

act of faith concerning the present in which we live: even today God's Spirit hovers over the abyss of darkness and formlessness that is our world. Like an invigorating wind he sweeps through our days.

Or:

The message we are now to hear is of the creation of the world. In it we experience the all-creating power of God that makes itself felt even more mightily in the days of redemption. After hearing the story, therefore, let us quietly ask God with all our heart to complete the saving work of creation by redeeming the entire world.

Or:

The first reading will be the hymn to creation. Everything comes from the hand of God, who has made all things good. Human beings are his images, made in order that they might praise him. Let us praise God for the goodness and beauty in the world; let us thank him for the love which he is constantly pouring out on us.

Second Reading (Sacrifice of Isaac)
Christ fulfills what is prefigured in the reading we are about to hear: "Christ has ransomed us with his blood, and paid for us the price of Adam's sin to our eternal Father" (Exsultet).

Third Reading (Exodus)
With thankful hearts let us listen to the story of the event heralded in the Exsultet: "This is the night when first you saved our fathers: you freed the people of Israel from their slavery and led them dry-shod through the sea. This is the night when the pillar of fire destroyed the darkness of sin."

Or:

We turn now to the story of the first Easter night. And when at the end of it we raise our voices in the song of praise which Moses sang along with the whole people, it becomes clear to us that what is narrated is not a purely past event but a reality we are constantly experiencing, namely, that Christ leads us safely through every danger and affliction.

Or:

Let us listen now to how God's power freed his people from slavery in Egypt. Let us reflect how through Christ, God has marvelously continued this work of liberation in our lives. After the reading, let us in silence ask God to show his power and make all human beings his people and his children.

Or:

God rescues his people from slavery. He leads them through the waters of liberation in order then to make a covenant with them at Sinai. In like manner the water of baptism has liberated us from the power of the Evil One so that we might live a new life. God be praised! We have been rescued and redeemed by the death and resurrection of Christ!

Fourth Reading (Promise of Return from Exile)
From the beginning what God wills is our salvation. What he does for us by his action of creation, he does again in the rescue from the flood; he does it again for Isaac at his sacrifice and for Israel at the crossing through the Red Sea to freedom; he does it still again when he rebuilds Jerusalem after its destruction and the exile of the people. He does it for us when he builds the future with us.

Sixth Reading (the Way to God)
The entire world has come forth from the hand of God, and everywhere we see the evidence of his loving care. But his wisdom also manifested itself among us in bodily form in Jesus Christ; the crucified and risen Jesus is "the way, the truth, and the life."

Seventh Reading (a New Heart of Flesh)
Wherever God acts, there is life. He did not abandon
his people to captivity and dispersal; he did not abandon his Son to death, but raised him to life. Neither
does he allow us to be destroyed, but grants us life and
a future.

Or:

Through the prophets God promises all human beings a
good future. He himself will intervene and make them
new. Let us thank him for raising us from the depths of
sin and sanctifying us by his Spirit.

BEFORE THE GLORIA
The hour is at hand when the Lord returns to his servants; if he finds us watching (along with the newly
baptized), he will invite us to his table. Therefore let us
now light the candles on the altar and jubilantly acclaim
Christ, the risen Lord, in the ancient hymn of praise,
the Gloria.

Or:

The hour is at hand for Christ to come among us, his
waiting servants and handmaids, and invite us to
celebrate the Easter meal with him. Therefore let us
light the candles on the altar and begin the song of
victory with which the angels greeted his entrance into
our world: Glory to God. . . .

Or:

God's will is that we be saved: that is the message in all
the pages of the Old Testament that we have been reading. This redemptive will of God has been "incar-
nated," "embodied," in Christ's incarnation, death,
and resurrection. Christ comes to us now and calls us to
his table and the reception of his body, so that through
baptism and communion we may become like him, the
crucified and risen one. We greet him now as risen

Lord, as the redeemer and lifegiver who is present in our midst: Glory to God. . . .

BEFORE THE EPISTLE (ROMANS 6)
We must suffer and die with Christ in our present life, so that we may also rise with him.

BEFORE BAPTISM
The doors of our parish church are now opening to admit the candidates for baptism at this Easter Vigil: NN. Let us accompany their procession to the font with our prayers, and let us pray as well for our entire community that the power of baptism may work effectively in every one of us.

Music Sources

GIA Publications, Inc. (GIA)
7407 S. Mason Ave.
Chicago, IL 60638

Worship II Hymnal
The Gelineau Gradual
ICEL Resource Collection
Alleluia and Psalm for Easter
  (Proulx)

North American Liturgy
  Resources (NALR)
2110 W. Peoria
Phoenix, AZ 85029

A Dwelling Place
Earthen Vessels (EV)

World Library Publications
  (WLP)
50640 N. Ravenswood
Chicago, IL 60640

Cantor Book

Augsburg Publishing House
426 S. Fifth St.
Minneapolis, MN 55415

Lutheran Book of Worship

Resource Publications
P.O. Box 444
Saratoga, CA 95070

The Psalm Locator

National Association of
  Pastoral Musicians
225 Sheridan Street, N.W.
Washington, DC 20011

Liturgy in Lent (Hansen)